Poised For Partnership:

How to successfully move from senior associate and senior manager to partner by building a cast-iron personal and business case for partnership

Heather Townsend

Excedia Group Ltd
The Forest Centre,
Station Road,
Marston Moretaine,
Bedfordshire.
MK43 0PR
Tel: + 44(0)1234 48 0123
www.excediagroup.co.uk

First published 2015 (print and electronic)

H2MP Publishing and The Excedia Group Ltd are not responsible for the content of third-party internet sites.

ISBN: 978-0-9932506-0-6 (Print)
          978-0-9932506-3-7 (PDF)

Praise for the book

❝ The jump from senior associate to partner can be huge and unfamiliar – this book is clear, practical and reassuring. It set me on the right route, at a solid pace, and gave me the courage to go for it. For someone who picked this book up along the way, Heather's ability to articulate the challenges facing a would-be partner is uncanny. Her step-by-step guide to overcoming those challenges is even better. Well worth the read"

FIONA HINDS, SENIOR ASSOCIATE HOWARD KENNEDY LLP

❝ I highly recommend Heather's new book Poised for Partnership as a must read for any Senior Manager, Senior Associate or Director who wants to take the step up to Partner. It has also been helpful to me in considering my firm's succession plan and the next generation of Directors."

JUDY DYKE, DIRECTOR AT TYNDALLWOODS

❝ This action-orientated and practical book expertly captures all the things which are crucial to making partner"

JOHN MOSS, JA CONSULTING

❝ This book is an invaluable aid to anyone considering the transition from associate to partner and employee to employer. Practical, thought-provoking and well-presented, the books allows you to dive in at any point, meaning that it is not just useful now, but will be for years to come."

KEVIN POULTER, LEGAL DIRECTOR BIRCHAM DYSON BELL LLP

❝ This is a great book which I recommend to anyone serious about making partner in a Big 4 firm. It's not easy going from being a fee earner with high chargeable targets to having your own client portfolio. This book gives you honest advice on how to go about making that transition."

ORLA POWER, SENIOR MANAGER, RISK ADVISORY EY

If Having made the somewhat daunting move from in house back to private practice with the primary aim of achieving partner, I am so grateful that I have found Heather Townsend and her books. This book has given me a clear structure upon which I can step up to the challenge, and with greater confidence than I might otherwise have had. This book is easy to read, I am certain this will help me immensely.

JONATHAN JAMES MORE, SENIOR ASSOCIATE

If Another excellent and highly relevant book from Heather Townsend. Achieving partnership is a two-way deal - between the aspirant and the firm and both parties must take responsibility in making it happen. This book sets out the template in a jargon free and practical manner and should be a 'must read' for both those that seek partner status and those primarily responsible for making the appointment."

PETER GILLMAN, EX-MANAGING DIRECTOR
OF PRICE BAILEY LLP

If The only person who can help you make partner ultimately is you. You have to be motivated to make the journey. However, this book will help guide you and provide you will invaluable tips and fantastic insight. Regardless of how much help your firm gives you, this is an essential read. There is no silver bullet when it comes to making partner, but this will do a damn good job of helping you get there if you act on the advice it contains. I really wish this book had been around when I was making the journey."

PHIL MULLIS, PARTNER AT WILKINS KENNEDY LLP

If If making partner feels like a long, winding and challenging journey, this book will be your SatNav, navigating you successfully to your destination. This book is brilliant, and I would highly recommend it."

DEV MODI, MANAGING DIRECTOR, THE OMEGA ACADEMY LTD

Contents

Introduction

❝ What is the recipe for successful achievement? To my mind there are just four essential ingredients: Choose a career you love, give it the best there is in you, seize your opportunities, and be a member of the team.

BENJAMIN FRANKLIN FAIRLESS

The toughest career transition you will ever make is the journey from senior associate/director through to partner. This isn't just another promotion. This is where you move from employee to business owner. Not only will you need to find the time to build your own practice, but also you will need to fundamentally change the relationships you have with your peers, partners and how you view your role going forward.

This book will be your secret weapon to successfully navigate the murky waters which lie ahead for you, as you take the final step up to partner. By reading this book and then taking action:

- You'll learn how to build such a compelling Business Case and Personal Case that your firm *has* to admit you to the partnership.

- The Partnership Panel Interview and pitching your Business Case will hold no fear for you

- You will know exactly what you need to say, demonstrate and prove to your partners to earn the right to join their exclusive club, and have *Partner* on your business card.

Terminology

Wherever possible I have tried to make this book as jargon free as possible. However, there are a few key words or phrases used consistently throughout the book.

Business Case: This is where you demonstrate to your partners the commercial advantage of making you a partner in the firm.

Personal Case: This is where you show to your partners that you think, feel and act at the standard expected of a partner in your firm.

Partner Track: The period of time, often between 0–3 years, when you decide to transition from senior associate/director to partner. Towards the end of the Partner Track you will start to go through the Partnership Admissions Process. Some firms will have a formal Partner Track process or programme where their high flyers will be groomed for partnership.

Partner Track Plan: Your overall plan to help you build a cast-iron Business Case and Personal Case to make partner.

Partnership Admissions Process: The formal or informal process that your firm uses to assess your suitability to be admitted to the partnership.

Partnership Vote: This is the last part of the Partnership Admissions Process where the partners all vote to decide who they will admit to the partnership.

Sponsoring Partner: The person in your firm who formally recommends that you should go through the Partnership Admissions Process. Without a strong recommendation from your Sponsoring Partner you are unlikely to be admitted to the partnership.

Junior Partner: The first grade of partner where most new partners begin.

Partner Panel Interview: This is a common part of many firm's Partnership Admissions Process. A panel of partners will interview candidates for partnership. During the interview candidates are often expected to present their Business and Personal Case for partnership.

Management Board: Most partnerships have the equivalent of a Board of Directors. The board may be called the 'Leadership Team', 'The Executive Team', 'The Board', or 'The Executive Leadership Group'. In this book it is referred to as the Management Board.

Partnership Selection Committee: This is a group of partners that the firm trusts to evaluate each candidate's Business Case and Personal Case, and recommend who they think is ready for partnership. In small firms the Partnership Selection Committee is very often the firm's Management Board.

Partnership Council: A Partnership Council is normally an elected set of representatives for the partners. Only the large firms tend to have a Partnership Council. Typically the Partnership Council will be used to review the effectiveness of the firm's leadership and management and has responsibility for partners' remuneration. The council is often used to ensure that appointments to the firm's leadership roles are handled effectively and in the right interests of the partnership.

What happens when you are on Partner Track?

No two firms operate in the same way. It is impossible to give a definitive timeline of what will happen to you as you go through Partner Track but diagram 0.1 will give you a good idea of what is likely to happen.

Get promoted to Senior Associate, Senior Manager or Director

Establish support team including Mentor and External Coach

Get on Partner Track and (optional) onto the firm's programme for people on Partner Track. You may or may not be told you are on Partner Track

Start building Business Case and Personal Case, i.e.

- Start to win own work to build a partner-sized client portfolio so that can feed self and team with work
- Start thinking, feeling and acting like a partner rather than senior employee of business
- Establish strong personal brand internally and externally in order to win own work and be noticed positively by partners
- Start due diligence on self and firm

Sponsoring Partners make recommendations who should be put through the Partnership Admissions Process

Formal Partnership Admissions Process starts

This could include:

- Written submission of Business and Personal Case
- Assessment Centre
- Partner Panel Interview and up to 6 interviews
- Psychometric assessments and verbal/numerical reasoning tests

Partnership selection committee make recommendations on who should be made up to partner

Partnership vote on who will be admitted to the partnership

New partner promotions announced internally and externally

- Final due diligence

Officially made up to partner. This is often at the start of your firm's financial year

1-3 years

Could be up to 9 months

Diagram 0.1: What will happen when you are on Partner Track

Why is it so tough to take the final step up to partner?

Many talented and often brilliant professionals have failed to make the final step up to partner. So, what makes it so tough?

- The recent recession and ongoing uncertainty in the global and local economies have put firms' profit margins under significant pressure. As a result firms are deliberately reducing their partner numbers to protect the size of their drawings.

- Partnerships now tend to expect their future partners to have a client following before being promoted to partner. As a result your Business Case and Personal Case need to be built on top of the demands of your day job.

- There are normally fewer partner vacancies available than the number of people going through the Partnership Admissions Process. This means that the admissions process is competitive. You are up against other great professionals in your firm.

- A firm will decide on how many partners they will admit in one year. This is hugely dependent on the health of the firm's finances and the confidence within the partnership. Consequently you are very much reliant on market forces. Your Partners have to be very confident in the strength of your Business Case before they will admit you to the partnership.

Having said all of this, it is still possible to make partner. It is not the chosen few or the lucky ones who get through to the partnership. The people who do achieve the holy grail of making partner are the ones who are prepared to 100% commit to becoming a partner, pace themselves by prioritising and working to a plan, go fully outside of their comfort zone, and build the right team of people around them to help them get to partner.

When should you start to build your Business Case and Personal Case for partnership?

It can often take years to build a truly cast-iron Business Case and Personal Case for partnership. After all, large, profitable pieces of juicy client work don't magically appear. Building a partner-sized client portfolio takes hard work, planning and focus. The earlier you start the process of building your Business Case and Personal Case for partner, the easier the Partnership Admissions Process will become.

A Magic Circle firm in the UK used to formally start to prepare their future partners just before they were about to go through the Partnership Admissions Process. After receiving feedback from their senior associates they now do this work 2–3 years before they expect an individual to go through the Partnership Admissions Process. They know that if their potential new partners are prepared to put the time and effort in the 2–3 years before going through the Partnership Admissions Process, then the process becomes more of a formality.

If you are reading this book and thinking that you want to make partner in the next 12 months, but haven't yet started to create your Business Case and Personal Case, don't worry. It is not impossible to make it successfully through the Partnership Admissions Process without 2–3 years of preparation behind you. This book will show you the shortcuts you can make, and what to prioritise to give yourself the best chance of making it through to partner this time around.

What do you need to stop doing right now to get noticed and increase your chances of making it successfully through the Partner Track?

Firstly, stop thinking that getting to partner will be inevitable. Very few professionals who get to senior associate/director actually make it to partner. In fact, the organisation Leadership Skills, led by Tara Fennessy found that only 2% of people make it through the promotions process to partner in a Big 4 firm. The people who do successfully make it put the work in. The days of 'waiting your turn' or thinking that you will 'get the tap on the shoulder' are now long gone. It won't be you going through the Partnership Admissions Process unless you start to put the work in to build your Business Case and Personal Case for partnership right now.

It can be very easy to put off your own career development. After all, there is always something to do when you are a senior associate or director. If you are going to really make it to partner you need to commit to your own development. As you will find out in Chapter 1, the first steps are to create your own motivating career goals and then build your Partner Track Plan.

You need to put your head above the parapet and tell your partners that you are incredibly serious and committed to making partner. Your technical skills will not do the talking for you. Too many talented professionals let their career plateau by assuming wrongly that doing a good job is enough to get them noticed and fast-tracked into the partnership. The sooner you put up your hand and say, metaphorically " *I'm in*" the more opportunities will come your way. Those people who are realistic about the work they need to do, will be the ones who start having the right conversations and involving the right people earlier.

Being on Partner Track can be a lonely business. However, you don't need to do it all yourself. You can drastically increase your chances by regularly asking for help from your support team. Chapter 3 in the book will show you who you need in your support team and the roles they will play.

It is only natural that at times along the way you will worry about whether you will get there or not. Worrying is unhelpful and wastes emotional energy, so prioritising, taking action and planning is the answer. This book will help the process feel a lot easier. There are plenty of people who can help you at every step of the way as you learn to feel, look and act like you belong around the partnership table.

How to tell your partners that you are serious about your intention to progress your career to partner

It can be hard to tell your partners that you want to go for partnership. When I interviewed several new partners a few years ago, they all vociferously agreed that the first step to make partner in your firm is to tell a partner. So, why do so many professionals recoil from the thought of doing this? I've heard people say things like this:

- *That's not the way it's done in my firm*
- *It's too early to think about going for partner*
- *I don't want to come across as pushy or arrogant*
- *I'm worried they wouldn't take me seriously*
- *I'm worried that they will tell me I'm not good enough*
- *I don't want my peers (or partners) to think I'm getting ideas above my station.*

If you agreed as you read through that list, remember that most of it is probably in your head. The best way to see whether you have any chance of making partner in your firm is to voice your career ambitions to your Supervisor.

Now, how to have that conversation? It's probably not advisable to announce in a pub, slightly tipsy (or very tipsy) that you want to become a partner. Neither is telling a room full of your peers that you want to be a partner the best way to have the conversation. Don't even think about getting someone else to talk to your partner about your partnership prospects – are you a man/woman or mouse? If you are going to be a successful partner, you must be prepared to have a courageous conversation.

Here is how to have this conversation. Firstly, arrange to have a private conversation with your supervisor or the partner you work with most often. If you are asked for a reason for the meeting, say it's about *how I am getting on in the firm* (or something like that). In the meeting, after some chit-chat, ask the partner a couple of questions:

- *How do you think I am performing?*
- *Where could I be improving or strengthening my skill set ready for the future?*
- *What do you think about my potential for progressing my career in this firm?*
- *What skills or capability would I need to gain if I wanted to make partner in this firm?*

Questions such as these will underscore that you are keen and committed to progressing to partner – and will also naturally lead onto an easy conversation about whether you want to get to partner.

Who is this book for?

This book is written for knowledge workers who are employed within a professional partnership and want to take the final step in their career to make partner. This includes lawyers, accountants, management consultants, architects, consulting engineers and surveyors. The book is also a useful guide for anyone outside of a professional partnership who would like to make the leap from industry into a partnership role.

Whilst the book primarily caters to the needs of experienced professionals who are on Partner Track and 0–3 years out from making partner, people responsible for talent management, leadership development and senior associate/director level development will also find this book invaluable.

If you are a senior associate, senior manager, director or head of a firm's practice management department, who wants to take the next step to make partner, this book will:

- Answer the burning, and often unanswered, question *What do I need to do to progress my career to partner around here?*

- Show you how to create a cast-iron Business Case and Personal Case for partnership, even if your firm doesn't have a formally communicated Partnership Admissions Process.

- Support you to pace yourself so you don't get burnt out before you have a shot at partner.

- Help you get noticed by the partners in your firm as a potential future partner.

- Give you tried and tested strategies to shine and progress successfully to the end of your firm's Partnership Admissions Process.

- Arm you with the right questions to check that partnership in your firm is 100% right for you.

- Help you to reduce the reputational and financial risks associated with making partner.

- Clearly show you what skills, attitudes, behaviours and experience you will need to demonstrate to rapidly progress to partner.

If you are currently in industry and wanting to join a professional partnership as a partner, this book will:

- Show you how to evidence a strong Business Case, even if you have no previous experience of selling services.

- Give you a guide for how to make yourself as attractive as possible to a partnership.

- Clearly show you what skills, attitudes, behaviours and experiences you will need to demonstrate to be recruited in at partner level in a professional services firm.

- Support you to reduce the reputational and financial risks associated with joining a partnership as a new partner.

- Arm you with the right questions to check that the partner role being offered is 100% right for you.

- Give you tried and tested strategies to shine and progress successfully to the end of your target firm's Partnership Admissions Process.

If you have picked up this book because you have been asked to help your own practice or advise a practice on leadership development, talent management and succession planning matters, you will find this book to be a jargon-free, rich source of advice.

At the moment, this book is the only widely available definitive guide to help people take the step up from senior associate/director to be formally admitted to the partnership. The book will become an invaluable, well read and scribbled on book for anyone responsible for talent management or succession planning within a professional practice.

How to use this book

This book can be used in two different ways. It can be read from cover to cover. Or you can use the Partner Track Self-Assessment Tool to see where you need to strengthen your Business Case and Personal Case for partnership. Then go to the relevant chapter to dip in and out of the book as you progress along the Partner Track. If this book is going to help you build a cast-iron Business Case and Personal Case for partnership don't ignore the exercises or questions it poses. No-one ever made it to Partner without going outside their comfort zone.

As you read through the book, it is time to be brave and make the time to answer the questions, and complete the action points in each chapter.

At the end of each chapter there are:

- actions for you to put into practice what you have just learnt; and

- links and references to further resources.

The Career Kitbag

 Throughout the book this symbol will show you where there is a resource in the Career Kitbag at http://www.howtomakepartner.com which will help you.

The Career Kitbag contains over 40 free and downloadable resources. These resources include plans, templates and guides, all designed solely to meet the needs of professionals in practice who want to progress their career.

The Partner Track Self-Assessment Tool

Before you go any further in this book, download your copy of the Partner Track Self-Assessment Tool and fill it out. Your results from the tool will help you prioritise which chapters you need to read first.

 The Partner Track Self-Assessment Tool is available to download in the Career Kitbag.

For each of the statements in the table rate yourself between 1 and 5. After you have finished rating yourself, prioritise reading the chapters where you have scored the lowest.

Creating the space, energy and desire to make it through Partner Track to Partner

Poor/Rarely = 1	Your score (1-5)	Excellent/Always = 5	Go to chapter
I haven't given my long-term career much thought. My main focus is getting through the day.	1 2 3 4 5	I know exactly where I want my career to be in 10 years time. I have detailed plans in place to help me get there, which are broken down into achievable and motivating milestones. I look at my career plan at least monthly. The actions I want to take for my career plan are included on my Weekly Planner.	Chapter 1
I am very concerned how I am going to achieve everything for my day job let alone what is needed to build a strong Business Case and Personal Case for partnership. I have not got a specific plan to help me through Partner Track or the Partnership Admissions Process, so my progress is sporadic at best.	1 2 3 4 5	I have built as part of my career plan a specific plan to enable me to get to partner. Within this plan I have identified my priorities and divided up what I need to achieve so I have paced myself appropriately. My Sponsoring Partner, Mentor and External Coach have reviewed and contributed to my plan. I am enthused and inspired to implement my plan and have already taken decisions and actions to make sure my Partner Track Plan gets achieved each week.	
I struggle to keep on top of everything at work, and I am often fire-fighting. My inbox is generally full, and I am not the best for returning calls. I am often getting feedback that I need to be more organised and structured at work.	1 2 3 4 5	I am known for being highly organised with my telephone and e-mail communications, plus filing. At the end of each day my inbox is reduced to zero, my desk is tidy, and I have a To Do list written for the next day, which allows me to switch off after I leave work. I am completely up-to-date with all my expenses, timesheets and reporting requirements.	Chapter 2
I operate on a reactive, fire-fighting basis each day, focusing on completing urgently important tasks first and working on high importance items whenever I can fit them in.	1 2 3 4 5	I operate according to a default calendar and prioritise my activities based on high importance items first and urgently important items second. My Weekly Planner includes urgent items as well as long-term important items for my career.	
I don't feel as if anyone in the firm cares about me or my career.	1 2 3 4 5	My partner, Mentor and Head of Department completely support and endorse my 3-year Career Plan. They are actively helping me to build my skill set and experience to achieve my short-, medium- and long-term career aims.	Chapter 3

I don't feel supported inside or outside of work, and assume that I need to get on and do it all myself.	1 2 3 4 5	I have a team of people inside and outside of work who support me to be my best inside and outside of work. These people include my Partner, Mentor, Head of Department, External Coach, 'life' partner, friends inside and outside of work.	Chapter 3
I have no aims for my life outside of work, and my work tends to stop me having time for anything other than work and sleep.	1 2 3 4 5	I have goals and milestones for my life outside of work. I am actively working on achieving these goals so that I feel like I have a meaningful life inside and outside of work. As a result of my focus on having a life outside of work, I would say that I am genuinely happy most of the time. I consciously make sure that I am making time for myself and key relationships outside of work.	Chapter 4
I am frequently ill and feel burnt out or highly stressed for much of the time. It is rare for me to get a good night's sleep and I rely on caffeine (and maybe other stimulants) to keep me going through the day.	1 2 3 4 5	I actively look after my mental, physical and spiritual health. I am rarely ill and am seen to have good physical strength. I have good energy levels and wake most mornings feeling refreshed and ready for the challenges ahead.	

Doing your research on you and your firm

I have not spent much, if any, time building my own self-awareness. I am often surprised by the feedback I am given.	1 2 3 4 5	Using data from psychometric profiling tools, 360° feedback, competency frameworks and performance reviews I have a good level of self-awareness and where my strengths and weaknesses are. I know I will be a good fit for partner in my firm.	Chapter 5
I don't know what my personal values are, and don't feel as if I fit in at work. I often have to compromise on what I feel is right, or what I want, to fit in with what my firm wants from me.	1 2 3 4 5	I know my personal values and how these guide me on a daily basis. My values are closely aligned to my firm and departmental values. I feel like I fit in at work and know that I am seen as one of the club.	
I have no passion for what I do, but don't know what I would do if I did something else.	1 2 3 4 5	I love my work, and feel proud of my firm. It is quite common for my work not to feel like work. I have great people working around me who I love working with.	

Statement	1 2 3 4 5	Statement	Chapter
How the firm is financed and its overall people, financial and marketing strategies are a mystery to me. No-one has yet taken the time to explain what I would be required to achieve as a junior partner.	1 2 3 4 5	I have been given full access to the firm's financial records and am clear on the financial risk I will be taking on if I decide to buy into the firm. I have got an external advisor to look through the firm's management accounts for the last 2 years. I know exactly how much support I will receive and what I will be required to do to hit my numbers and progress into the partnership.	Chapter 6

Creating a persuasive and compelling Business Case for partnership

Statement	1 2 3 4 5	Statement	Chapter
I have not got a Business Case for partnership.	1 2 3 4 5	I have been working on my Business Case for the last 1–3 years, and have the backing of my Sponsoring Partner, Mentor, Head of Department and other key stakeholders in the firm. I have got opinions and ideas for my Business Case from key stakeholders in the partnership.	Chapter 7
I am yet to really build my own client following. If I have a client following, it is not important to the firm.	1 2 3 4 5	I have built a partner-sized client portfolio, and if I left the firm, most of this portfolio would come with me. The portfolio is strategically important to the firm.	
Key account management for my clients is rarely done at all. There are no relationship plans in place for key clients. Clients are rarely, if at all, categorised.	1 2 3 4 5	All clients have been categorised, and service levels delivered based on the client category. Key accounts have been identified and each key account has a proactive key account plan, relationship plans and the plans are helping gain a greater slice of the client's business. Client portfolio analysis is being proactively completed.	
I do not have a marketing plan to produce a predictable number of leads, improve conversion rates, increase the average revenue per transaction and increase the transactions per client. The results of spending on marketing and advertising are unmeasured and unmanaged. Any revenue growth is largely down to luck.	1 2 3 4 5	I have an aggressive, measurable marketing plan to produce a predictable number of leads, improve conversion rates, increase the average revenue per transaction, and increase the transactions per client so profits increase significantly. Results of the marketing plan are being measured and improved on a weekly basis.	

Client service standards and processes, if in place, are not automatically followed.	1 2 3 4 5	I make sure my team members are committed to deliver extraordinary client service. Our client proposition is tailored to each client, and there are processes and systems in place to make sure we deliver and delight each client. My current client base regularly recommends my team and me to the right type of client.	Chapter 7
It is very difficult to distinguish between my peers and myself. I have not taken the time to truly develop a niche, and are more concerned with how to make myself as attractive as possible to as many clients as possible.	1 2 3 4 5	I am known as the Go-To Expert for a technical or sector specialism, both inside and outside of the firm. I am regularly consulted for my specialist expertise and often get quoted in industry, local and national press. If you did a Google search for me you would instantly get how I help my clients. I am able to charge premium rates for my time compared to my peers. As a result of my external market-facing profile, I regularly bring in opportunities for others in the firm.	
I may have a LinkedIn profile. When I network, I mostly focus all my efforts on face-to-face networking. My on-line presence is limited to my bio on the firm's website.	1 2 3 4 5	I have an active on-line presence where I regularly engage with my clients, prospects and introducers. My LinkedIn profile is fully completed and a great shop window for what I do. I regularly write about what I do on the firm blog and/or my LinkedIn profile (as part of the LinkedIn publisher function). My profile is viewed at least once a day by potential introducers and clients. I interact daily with my network on social media.	Chapter 8
I don't have a Content Plan, and rarely produce any content.	1 2 3 4 5	I have thought about what type of content I need to produce to help engage my ideal client at each stage of their buying journey. I have a Content Plan and regularly produce different types of content on schedule. My content is regularly read/listened to by the type of people I want to meet and engage with. The content I produce and share helps me generate the right amount of leads, reduce my client's time to buy and increase my conversion rate.	
I have not yet had the opportunity to build up my own networks of introducers.	1 2 3 4 5	I maintain regular communication with a close network of introducers who regularly refer and recommend me to my ideal clients. I am equally proactive at helping them achieve their business and career aims. I have a formal plan to keep in touch with my best introducers. I use both face-to-face and on-line tools to help keep me top-of-mind with my network of introducers.	Chapter 9

Statement (left)	Rating	Statement (right)	Chapter
I spend little, if any, time working on building and nurturing my network. I very often turn up at events without a purpose for being there. My LinkedIn profile is pretty empty and if I use Twitter or Facebook it is for personal reasons only.	1 2 3 4 5	I am actively working on building and nurturing a network, which will help me achieve my short-, medium- and long-term, goals and milestones. I use both on-line and off-line networking tools to help me achieve my networking aims. I have a daily, weekly, monthly and quarterly Networking Routine to help me keep my network warm and supportive.	Chapter 9

Becoming a 'member of the club'

Statement (left)	Rating	Statement (right)	Chapter
I have a limited or non-existent fan base from the partners, and most partners would be surprised to hear that I am keen to go for partnership. I am not known outside of my practice area. I am not sure whether I have the support of the lead partner of my practice area.	1 2 3 4 5	I have built a reputation within the partnership where I am already seen and viewed as a partner, or 'one of them'. I have been told I am on Partner Track. The skill set, strengths and talents, which I bring to the partnership, are recognised and wanted by the partners. I have a large and wide fan base in the partnership, with many partners actively pushing for me to be made up to partner. I am well known outside of my practice area and have spent time working in other offices throughout the firm.	Chapter 10
I often receive feedback that I need to work on my profile. It's not uncommon for me to find that I am scrambling about for work. I sometimes feel as if I am at the bottom of the list to get picked for an assignment.	1 2 3 4 5	I am a high profile and visible member of my firm and department. People regularly talk about me as 'one to watch' and 'partnership potential'. Partners and managers actively try to get me to work with their clients. Clients regularly ask for me to work on their stuff.	
I don't yet have the confidence or presence that a partner needs. Most people tell me I need to work on my gravitas and executive presence if I am to gain the respect of my peers, team and generate more of my own work.	1 2 3 4 5	People inside and outside of the firm treat me as if I am a partner. When I talk people listen to me and give me the level of respect that partners in the firm are due. People from outside the firm are often surprised to find I am not a partner yet.	Chapter 11
The team around me do not support my career path to make it to partner. They are likely to protest, leave or make my life difficult if I get made up to partner.	1 2 3 4 5	My team fully support my career aspiration to make partner.	

		Chapter 11
I (and my team) am struggling to hit our targets and numbers. Our Business Development efforts are struggling to bring in the right clients at a profitable fee level.	1 2 3 4 5	My team and I regularly hit our financial and billing targets. I (supported by my team) am hitting and exceeding my new business target. Clients are invoiced promptly, and every member of my team has a chargeable time target as well as a WIP and Lockup target.
I rarely delegate to members of my team, and find that I spend too much of my time helping sort out conflict and problems with my team. On the rare occasions I do delegate to my team I find that the work comes back sub-standard and I need to often re-work it.	1 2 3 4 5	I have an incredibly supportive high performing team who are able to get the work done to a high standard with minimal intervention from me. I trust the team and regularly delegate work to them to allow me to focus on higher value work and winning more work from clients
No plan exists to identify and intentionally develop the talent within my team. Development for my team members happens on a haphazard basis, often based on who shouts loudest. There would be a big gap in my team if I got admitted to the partnership. I don't have a successor for me in my current role.	1 2 3 4 5	A plan to identify and intentionally develop emerging managers and leaders is carefully monitored by myself. Each member of my team has a personal development plan to help them perform and develop in the short, medium and long term. I regularly sit down with each member of my team to talk about their performance and development. A successor has been identified for my role when I get admitted to the partnership.
There is no rhythm of regularly scheduled team meetings and the communication from team members and stakeholders is inconsistent and inefficient. Off-site planning meetings are rare and decisions are communicated haphazardly throughout the team and department.	1 2 3 4 5	A rhythm of regularly scheduled team meetings for goal setting, reporting and accountability take place on an annual, quarterly, weekly and daily basis. Decisions made by senior people in the team and key stakeholders cascade quickly and easily through the team.
If difficult conversations happen at all, they rarely go well. There are high levels of WIP and Lockup, and debtor days are very high.	1 2 3 4 5	Timely feedback (both positive and negative) is regularly given to all individuals in the team. Critical feedback is always given sensitively and in private. Difficult conversations with clients – particularly billing matters – happen promptly and successfully.

There is little or no awareness of personality differences. Irritating communication patterns continuously plague the team and conflicts remain unresolved. A culture of frustration with the unadapted behavioural style of other team members exists.	1 2 3 4 5	The team has embraced a system for understanding and maximising the inherent synergies of personality differences. Communication is healthy and conflicts are resolved easily as team members adapt to the behavioural style of other team members.	Chapter 11

The final stages of Partner Track

I plan to sort out my pitch the week before my partnership interviews. I know I need to make time to practise and hone my Business Case pitch, but know I wouldn't have the time to do this justice. The slides for my pitch, if I have any, are mostly 'cut and pasted' sentences from my Business Case for partnership.	1 2 3 4 5	I have practised many times my Business Case pitch for partnership, and am now word perfect. My pitch is a condensed version of my Business Case with key parts of my Personal Case interwoven within the pitch. Every word included on my slide deck has been carefully crafted so there are no wasted words or unqualified/non-evidenced statements. I have practised my pitch and panel interview questions with a combination of Sponsoring Partner, Mentor and External Coach.	Chapter 12
I have never really considered these three questions, let alone have answers to them. • *Why should I be admitted to the partnership?* • *Why should I be admitted this time around to the partnership?* • *What is the risk to the business of not promoting me this time around?*	1 2 3 4 5	I can clearly and distinctly answer the questions: • *Why should I be admitted to the partnership?* • *Why should I be admitted this time around to the partnership?* • *What is the risk to the business of not promoting me this time around?* I have consulted with my Mentor and other influential partners to get the answers to these questions just right.	
The Partnership Admissions Process is a complete mystery to me. I have not prepared for any of the stages in the process and am relying on my ability to do my best on the day.	1 2 3 4 5	I know exactly what will happen to me throughout the Partnership Admissions Process. I have prepared for each element of the process and taken my time to get to know my interviewers wherever possible.	

PART I

Creating the space, energy, time and desire to make it to partner

Successfully getting through the long slog that is Partner Track requires a solid foundation. It is this firm foundation, which gives you the space, energy, time and desire to create the best Business Case and Personal Case possible.

In this part of the book, we consider how to create this firm foundation by:

- Creating your Partner Track Plan
- Finding the time to fit in all the extra demands on your time that being on Partner Track brings
- Forming a support team
- Keeping your mind and body healthy

1

Creating and writing your own Partner Track Plan to make it to partner

Topics covered in this chapter:

- What needs to be in your Partner Track Plan
- How to create your Partner Track Plan
- How to balance your workload to make it through Partner Track
- The importance of gaining feedback from others

❘❘ Developing the plan is actually laying out the sequence of events that have to happen for you to achieve your goal.

GEORGE L. MORRISEY

Look back on your career to date. I suspect that as your career has progressed you have significantly increased the demands on your time both inside and outside of work. As a non-partner your primary focus has been on client service and working with your partner to deliver to the clients' satisfaction. However, building a successful Business Case and Personal Case for partner means you now need to be seen to be actively bringing in new business and taking part in the day-to-day management of the firm. As if this wasn't enough, you will still be expected to hit your chargeable time targets. After all, very few firms can afford for their most expensive fee earners to become unprofitable in the years that they are on Partner Track. As a result, the challenge that everyone on Partner Track faces is how to create the time to build a compelling Business Case and Personal Case.

In this chapter we explore how to find the time to still fulfil your day-to-day responsibilities whilst carving out more time to build up your own client following and how to develop a team to support you.

What needs to be in your Partner Track Plan

Your Partner Track Plan is what will keep you literally on track to achieve your career aim of being voted into the partnership. Given the many demands on your time when you are on Partner Track, it can be so easy to lose focus on what is important to you right now. This is where your Partner Track Plan comes in.

There are multiple parts to your plan. What goes in your plan will be personal to your own particular circumstances. However, it is likely to contain all or some of the following parts:

Business development plan:

This is used to show your partners that you are able to build and maintain a partner-sized profitable client portfolio. It is likely to contain:

- Your personal marketing plan to attract new clients
- Key account plans to grow your current client portfolio and generate work-winning opportunities for other people in the firm
- A Networking Strategy to build strong Referral Networks, grow your profile and extend your reach
- Relationship plans for your key contacts
- Your pipeline and what you need to do to progress each opportunity so that it becomes a client.

Internal PR campaign plan:

When it comes to the Partnership Vote you want every partner to say *yes* to you becoming a partner in the firm. This means that they need to know who you are, respect you and feel that you are already thinking and acting like a partner. Your internal PR campaign plan is likely to contain:

- A stakeholder map of the key movers and shakers in your partnership and how you intend to positively influence and engage with them
- An activity plan to grow your profile across the firm.

Personal development plan:

The skill set needed by partners in a firm is very different to non-partners. For example, most people find that running a business is a skill set that needs to be learnt rather than something that comes naturally to them. This part of your plan is likely to contain:

- How you will gain the skill set and experience to be seen to be acting as if you are already a partner.
- Identification of your weaknesses and strengths, and how you will capitalise on your strengths and mitigate your weaknesses.
- How you will actually get the time to recharge and keep your energy high.

Team development plan:

You are unlikely to make it to partner without the support of a team behind you. After all, you don't want your own partnership ambitions to be jeopardised by the lack of successor to take over your current workload! This part of your plan is likely to contain:

- Individual development plans for your team
- A development plan for your whole team to engage them in your personal vision for the future.

Short-term 90-day action plan:

With so many plans to keep an eye on, it can be easy to forget about the action steps in one of the plans. Your short-term 90-day action plan will be where you condense all of your plans into one document detailing what you need to do and achieve in the next 30, 60 and 90 days.

Within the Career Kitbag are downloadable templates for all parts of the Partner Track Plan, with full instructions for how to use them

How to create your Partner Track Plan

Start with the end in mind

If you don't know where you're going, any road will get you there.

LEWIS CARROLL

Let's get serious now. When do you want to be made up to partner? This year? Next year? Within 5 years? Before you can put a plan together to create your Business Case and Personal Case for partnership, you need to know what you have to demonstrate, evidence or achieve before you will be recommended for partnership. This information will help you form the Goals you need to achieve to make partner.

Having clarity about Goals allows you to decide whether something is, or is not, a priority; i.e. do you need to invest time in this?

Goal setting will focus your acquisition of knowledge and help you to organise your time and resources so that you can make it to partner. Your self-confidence will improve as you achieve your Goals. Telling other people about your Goals is an excellent way of committing yourself into action.

The difference between Goals, Milestones and Objectives

Goals: These are what you want to achieve in the future, and are focused on your life inside and outside of work

Milestones: These are sub-goals, which if achieved will help you realise your Goals

© HEATHER TOWNSEND

Objectives: These are the specific, measurable actions you will do to accomplish your Milestones

Don't confuse good intentions with action. It can be very easy to delay writing your Partner Track Plan. After all, there is always something more pressing to do. In my experience, there will never be a right time to get started. If you are serious about making it onto and through Partner Track to partner, the time to take action is now. Merely saying you want something, won't make it happen

Case study: Clarice

Clarice decided she wanted to make partner by the time she was 40. After working with her coach, she set the following goals as part of her Partner Track Plan:

- *Business Development:* Build my client portfolio so it is worth £750,000 to the firm by Dec 31st 2015

- *Internal PR Campaign:* Have at least 30% of the equity partners backing my application for partnership by Dec 31st 2015

- *Personal Development:* Be performing at the level expected of a junior partner as set out in the firm's competency framework by Dec 31st 2015

- *Team Development:* My team will be highly supportive of me and able to service the client work I delegate to them without me needing to be involved by Dec 31st 2015

How to find out what you need to do to make partner, when no-one knows what you need to do

Many firms, including some very large Top 50 UK-based accountancy and legal firms, do not have a formal or structured process to get to partner. This is both a blessing and a curse! Even if your firm selects and votes on future partners in total secrecy, without their future partners even knowing they are being voted into the partnership, there are certain standards that you will need to achieve. These are:

- Demonstrate or show strong potential that you can grow and profitably manage a partner-sized client portfolio
- Be trusted to run and own a slice of the firm
- Be able to lead and develop a team to service the work you win
- Work harmoniously with the firm's existing partners
- Exhibit long-term commitment to the firm and its Values and Vision for the future.

Setting your priorities

Given the magnitude of the task ahead of you, it is not uncommon, like Clarice in our example, to have identified multiple Goals to get to partner in your ideal timeframe. Sometimes having many goals can overwhelm you and stop you from achieving any of them because you don't have the time to invest in any of them properly. Giving each of your Goals a priority level can help you focus on what is more important to start progressing earlier. For example, if your ideal client is a large multinational company you are likely to have a long sales cycle. If you are in that situation it makes sense for you to prioritise your business development related Goals ahead of working on your Personal Case for partnership.

Converting Goals into Milestones

Big Goals can be very daunting. It's only when you break them down into smaller more achievable sub-goals – Milestones – that you will find the motivation to start working towards your Goals.

There are many different ways of chunking down large Goals into smaller Milestones. To help you identify your Milestones, give yourself a quiet 30 minutes and the space to think by removing distractions from around you. For each of your Goals break them down into Milestones and attach a timeframe to each. You may find it helpful to write these down using a spreadsheet, calendar or Gantt chart.

Case Study: Sarah (Part 1)

Sarah had a Goal to build three Referral Networks which would bring her and the firm new business. She split this Goal into the following Milestones:

3-month Milestone

- Physically meet at least 10 people who would be able and willing to refer me work from manufacturing clients

6-month Milestone

- Have identified the members of my three Referral networks
- Received my 1st referral to a new manufacturing client from my three Referral Networks

1-year Milestone

- Generate £75k of new client work for the firm from my three Referral Networks

2-year Milestone

- Generate £250k of new client work for the firm from my three Referral Networks

 Use the Career Kitbag's Goal, Milestone and Objective Planner, to record your Goals, Milestones and Objectives to achieve each Goal.

Converting Milestones into Objectives

Now that you have identified your Milestones to enable you to achieve your Goals, it is time to turn them into specific, measurable, shorter-term Objectives, which identify *what* you need to do to achieve your Milestones within the desired timeframe.

Case Study:
Sarah (Part 2)

Sarah, took her 3-month Milestone and decided on her Objectives to help her achieve this Milestone.

- By 30th January identify at least three conferences, forums or networking groups where decision makers in manufacturing companies network.

- By 28th February complete my research to find Audit, Corporate Finance and Tax professionals in local accountancy firms who specialise in manufacturing companies

- By 15th February meet with my Mentor to pick her brains for who she thinks I should be talking with to find members for my Referral Networks

Some tips on effective Objective setting:

- Write your Objectives as a single sentence, containing what you want to do to achieve your Milestones

- Write them down and share them with other people

- Review them every three months

- Make sure you include a timeframe; e.g. weekly or 'by this date'

- Check that they are realistic and measurable.

How to balance your workload to make it through Partner Track

Every time I have spoken to someone who has successfully made the jump to partner, they tell me about the focus and dedication that it takes. To be focused means you need to know your Goals and what you want to achieve in the short, medium and long term. If you have these Goals and road maps of how you will build a cast-iron Business Case and Personal Case for partnership, you are then able to evaluate each opportunity against these – *will they help me achieve them or not?* You can then turn down the opportunities that will distract you from achieving your career aim of becoming partner.

Prioritise your development

At present, your diary is undoubtedly filled with fee-paying client work. In order to advance your career, you now need to add a new client which is YOU. Pursuing your own development requires time allocation, so treating your Partner Track Plan as an additional client is basically giving yourself permission to devote chunks of time to accomplish the necessary development work. To the extent that you can, assigning chunks of diary time to your Partner Track Plan should be done within your regular working hours, because from your perspective, the Plan is valid work, which leads to a future benefit for you.

Case Study: Mike

Mike was a senior associate in a Top 50 UK law firm. He had high billable targets to hit and was in demand from partners to help them with their clients. This was stopping him going out and developing his own client base and increasing the number of 'matters originated' that would be credited to him. He decided to set aside Monday morning for business development. He built himself a 'must do' routine for his weekly business development tasks. As a result of this level of focus on business development he found that his leads and matters originated doubled within six months.

Pace yourself

Making the transition to partner from senior associate/director is really a marathon not a sprint. Therefore, be honest with yourself and take it one small step at a time. We tend to over-estimate what we can get done in the short term and under-estimate what we can do in the long term. Putting one foot in front of another at a steady pace is what is going to get you to partner in one piece.

Create time to review progress

It is too easy to always be looking towards the next thing you need to achieve. However, being on Partner Track is a time for incredible personal growth and change. Therefore, it is important that you set aside time to review what you have learnt, and what you need to focus on in the next 90 days. It is a good idea to put aside some time every month, potentially with your Sponsoring Partner, Mentor or External Coach, to do this.

Summary

The hardest part of making partner is finding the time to build a strong Business Case and Personal Case for partnership. Using a Partner Track Plan, which you review regularly, will help you create the focus and discipline to still hit your numbers whilst building a compelling case for partnership.

Setting yourself Goals will help you commit to what you want to achieve. Breaking down these Goals into smaller more manageable Milestones, will make these more achievable. Progress, which helps to build confidence and momentum, will be more visible when you identify Milestones and Objectives to achieve these Goals.

Action Points

1. Write a first draft of your Partner Track Plan using the downloaded template from the Career Kitbag:

    1. Decide when you would ideally want to make partner

    2. Turn this into your Business Development, Internal PR Campaign, Personal Development, Team Development Goals and non-work related Goals

    3. Using the results of the Partner Track Self-Assessment Tool, identify your short- and medium-term priorities

    4. Break down your Goal to make partner into Milestones

    5. To achieve your first Milestones, create your 3-month Objectives

    6. Write these Objectives into your Weekly Planner.

2. Block out regular chunks of time in your diary to work on and review your Partner Track Plan

Further resources

BOOKS

For more advice on goal setting and planning, I recommend these books:

- *Eat That Frog!: Get More of the Important Things Done – Today!*, Brian Tracy, ISBN 978-1444765427

- *The 7 Habits of Highly Effective People*, Stephen R. Covey, ISBN 978-0684858395

WEBSITES

- Free Partner Track Plan template and instructions how to build your Partner Track Plan: http://www.howtomakepartner.com

2

How to find the time to create your business and personal case

Topics covered in this chapter:

- Common time leaks when on Partner Track
- How to adopt the right mindset to get the day job done and create the time to build your Business Case and Personal Case for partnership
- How to stop distractions and interruptions, such as phone calls and e-mails from limiting your daily productivity
- How to stop meetings from eating up your day
- How to delegate effectively

❲❲ Lack of direction, not lack of time, is the problem. We all have 24-hour days.

ZIG ZIGLAR

In the first chapter we explored the fundamental difficulty involved in the transition to partner: how to still hit your numbers whilst carving out time to build your Business Case and Personal Case for partnership. In fact, for a few years you are going to have two jobs: The day job, and then your extra job to build your own practice to demonstrate your readiness for partnership. This means you are going to have to manage your time very carefully. This chapter will give you some thoughts about how you will actually get everything done.

What are the most common time leaks when on Partner Track?

Of course, you can't actually leak time. However, you can waste time both intentionally and unintentionally, which will cause you to be ineffective or unproductive. Here are the most common 'time wasters' for people on Partner Track:

Networking for networking's sake

When you are told you need to start to bring in your own work, what is the first thing you do? Go networking. Of course, done well networking is one of the best ways to grow your profile and generate new business. If you haven't taken the time to really consider why you are networking, the brand you want to build, and the people you need in your network, you may as well have not gone out networking in the first place. Chapter 8 and 9 of this book will help make sure your networking is fit for purpose.

Poor management of junior staff

Continual disruptions, poor quality work, too much time spent reworking, are some of the most common complaints I hear about junior staff. Most of these complaints don't stem from poor quality junior staff. They stem from a lack of good management of your team. Chapter 11 will help you polish your people management skills and build a high quality team who you can trust beneath you.

Learning to say "no"

When you are trying to build a high internal and external market value it can be tempting to think that you have to say "*yes*" to everyone. The reality of the situation is that you will always have partners or team members asking you for things or members of your network wanting to meet you for coffee. Too much "*yes*" can easily lead to overwhelm or not having enough time to do the things that really matter. The best ways to gracefully decline involve:

- Helping them find a solution without using you, e.g. *"have you tried using...?"*

- Explaining your time constraints and finding out if they have any flexibility on timescales or how they want things to be done.

- Using your secretary to manage your diary and act as a gatekeeper for people who want to meet you.

- Offering to help them a little but not the whole hog, e.g. *"No, I can't do that, but I can do this."*

- Ask for time to think about it. You may find that the request goes away or you find a way to fulfil the request in a way that works for you and the other party.

Lack of delegation or poor delegation skills

If you are going to expand the amount of time you have to build your practice you will need to learn to delegate well to more junior staff. Delegation, and how to do it well, is explored fully at the end of this chapter.

Not knowing what you need to do to build your personal and business case

There is often a huge amount of mystery and conjecture about exactly what it takes to make partner in a firm. This can result in heartache and frustration, leading to procrastination, delays or mistakes being made on the way to making partner. Frequently, many people on Partner Track feel, often wrongly, that they can't ask the right questions to find out exactly what they need to do to make it to partner. The best way to avoid this happening to you is to assume that there is no wrong question, and seek out the right information and best source of advice you can find. This is why I recommend in the next chapter that you build a support team around you, which includes a Mentor and External Coach.

It is all about your mindset

I could share any number of productivity tools and apps, but at the end of the day being productive and efficient is all about your mindset and how you approach your working day, week and month. After all, no phone app or to-do list tool can actually make you physically use them.

To help you get into the right mindset to create the time to progress your career along Partner Track, consider these questions:

- What more could I do on my Partner Track Plan by being more organised?
- What would my family, friends and the people around me gain by me being more organised?
- How many business development opportunities am I not getting to by not managing my time more effectively?
- How much quicker would I get through Partner Track if I were able to fit more into less time?

Using a default diary

How to find the time to do business development when you have a full caseload is one of the typical challenges anyone on Partner Track faces. One of the productivity tools I suggest to people on Partner Track is to use a default diary.

This is where you have a standard daily, weekly, monthly, quarterly routine, which is timetabled permanently into your diary. This makes sure that the important (but often non-urgent) stuff, such as business development and meetings with your team members happen. For example, one of our clients used to block out every Friday morning as her time to work on her Partner Track Plan. See Diagram 2.1 for how she set up her default diary.

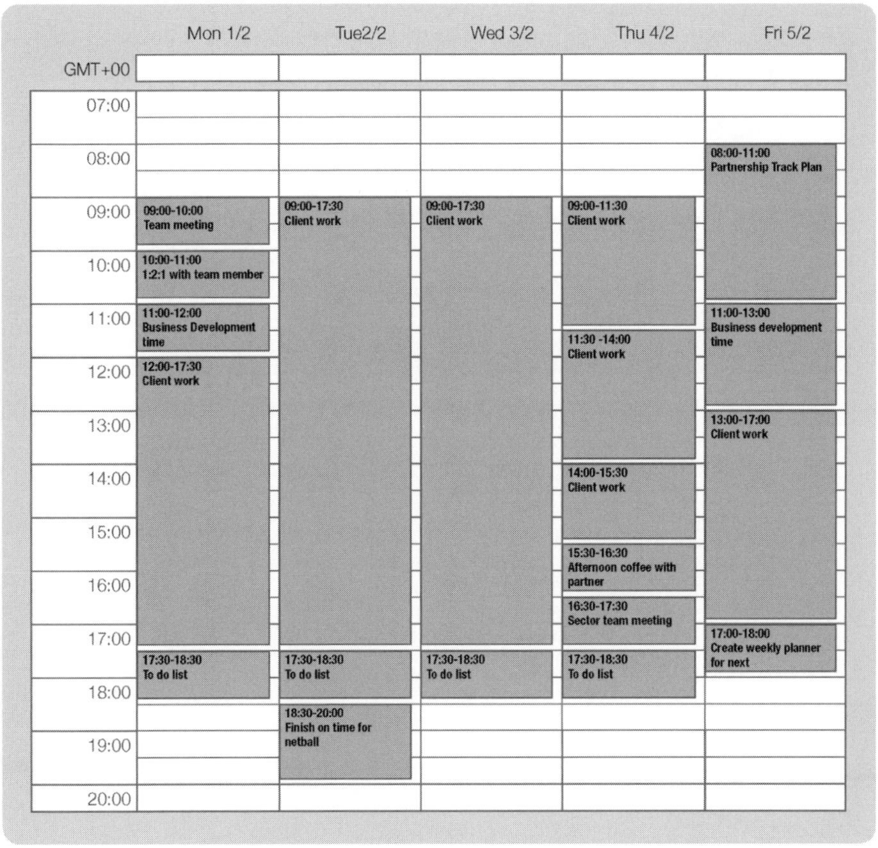

Diagram 2.1: Example of a default calendar

Prioritise, prioritise, prioritise

When you are on Partner Track it can seem like everything is important AND urgent. After all you still have client work to do, as well as a raft of extra responsibilities such as supervision, networking and building your profile with your partners. This means that you need to become ruthless at prioritising. I.e. being focused on the right thing to do now as well as the important stuff in the future. Using a Weekly Planner to help you timetable into your diary your priority tasks will help you never lose sight of what you really need to achieve in a week.

WEEKLY PLANNER	Week no: 47			From: November 30th		To: December 6th	
Mon	Tue	Wed	Thurs	Fri	Sat	Sun	
Business development, networking, people management and client service actions to complete							
Appraisal for Suzy			Finish reviewing audit report for HGR audit	Keeping-in-touch calls			
Partnership Track Plan tasks to complete							
	Meeting with my mentor		Meeting with Head of finance to go through the partnership annual reports	Partnership Track Plan review			
Any other actions to complete							
Departmental monthly meetings							

Your 3 Critical Results this Week - What You *Must* Achieve this Week	Done
Meeting with my mentor to discuss the 1st draft of my marketing plan for next quarter	
Evening out with my wife for date night	
Finish reviewing audit report for HGR audit	

Objectives for the month (taken from Partnership Track Plan)	Done
Finalise my marketing plan for the next quarter	
Supervise my managers to finish the audit reports due this month	
Agree on date nights and family activities with my wife	
Agree sector marketing plan for the environmental sector team	

Diagram 2.2: Your Weekly Planner, with critical results identified for the week

 Use the Career Kitbag's Weekly Planner template to help keep you focused on what you have to achieve each week

How to stop procrastination from sabotaging your success

Everyone from time to time will suffer from procrastination. Unfortunately procrastination is one of the ways that we actually sabotage our own success and potentially our partnership ambitions. For whatever reason, when we start to procrastinate, we put barriers and obstacles in the way of what we need to do. Dr Ferrari found that there are three types of procrastinators:

- Avoiders, who may be avoiding the task because of fear of failure, fear of success or because they are worried about what other people think

- Decisional procrastinators who struggle to make a decision, often because then they don't need to take responsibility for the outcome of the decision
- Thrill-seekers who are energised by a last minute rush and panic.

Here are 10 ways in which you can stop procrastinating:

- Identify why you are procrastinating. What can you do to overcome this reason?
- Be brave and just take the decision. Not taking a decision can very quickly become a mistake on our part.
- Break the task up in smaller and more manageable pieces
- Schedule some time with your External Coach or Mentor to explore why you are procrastinating
- Use and complete your To Do list, e.g. your weekly planner
- Set yourself deadlines which you must hit
- Get the difficult stuff out of the way first
- Aim to avoid striving for perfection
- Delegate or outsource
- Set aside an hour where you turn off all distractions and power through your To Do list.

Stopping e-mail dominating your day

One of the features of being on Partner Track is often an over-flowing inbox. There are all the emails you are cc'ed on from your team, the social media notifications, the circulated reports as well as the essential client emails to tackle. Here are 6 ways in which you can tame your inbox:

- Set times of the day when you will process your email
- Use email rules to do some of the email processing for you, e.g. setting up a folder called "invoices to process"

- Use email flags to make sure you don't lose an important email

- Unsubscribe from all unnecessary newsletters

- Get into the habit of actioning, filing or deleting an email immediately

- Give yourself a personal limit for the maximum amount of email your inbox can contain.

Minimising your interruptions and distractions

Have you ever got to the end of the day and just felt you couldn't get anything done because of phone calls, people stopping by or being messaged on the firm's instant chat system? Being able to guard and protect your quality thinking and working time is essential for anyone on Partner Track. Unfortunately the nature of working with clients and leading assignments means that interruptions and distractions are something that needs to be actively managed.

Here are some ideas to stop interruptions destroying your productivity e.g.

- If it's urgent and important, deal with it straight away

- Try standing up when the other person comes towards you. This will naturally shorten any disruption as the other person can't sit down and get comfortable.

- If the interruption has come at a bad time, reschedule it.

- Turn off the firm's instant messaging system and any social media or email notifications

- If you have your own office, shut your door when you don't want to be interrupted

- Save up your phone calls or follow up conversations so you can do them in a block of time

- Tell people when it is a good time to contact you

- If your firm allows you to do this, switch your phone onto voicemail or divert to your secretary.

Stopping meetings from eating up your day

Meetings are a necessary evil for someone in professional services. When you are on Partner Track there will always be someone who wants you to attend a meeting. This could be a staff, project related or committee meeting, a catch-up or a 'good' networking opportunity. As with all these things, balance is key. Yes, you want to make sure that your face is seen in the right places (see Chapter 10) but you still need to get the day job done. Only you can decide what meetings you need to actually attend. The best way to do this is look at your Goals, Milestones and Objectives. Will being present at this meeting help you with these? Or is it a pleasant distraction, which you can absent your-self from?

Delegation

❝ If it can be delegated, it must be. Never work on something that someone less experienced than you can do – your career will be on hold and you'll become more and more obsolete with each passing day.

DAVID MAISTER

If you are going to free up your time to build your business and per-sonal case, then you need to be able to delegate to a more junior and cheaper member of the firm. For example, the next time you are at a client meeting see if you can take a junior member of the team with you. The junior gets valuable exposure to a client meeting, and you get someone to take notes and complete the attendance note from the meeting.

If we don't have competent people to delegate to, then very often we will take the view that it's quicker and simpler to keep the work rather than delegate it down. In fact, in the last week alone two of my clients have stated that a lack of junior staff to delegate to will hamper their attempts to build their Business Case.

Whilst you may not always have access to competent junior staff to assist you on your client work or instructions, most of us have access to support staff. For example, it takes time to make sure you speak to the right people in your network at the right time. Why not ask your secretary or team PA to support you to get all your networking meetings in the diary?

Don't always assume that what you delegate will be done to your personal standard or right first time, particularly if you are delegating to a very inexperienced member of the team. Therefore, make sure that you allow enough time for any necessary briefing, rework or review time.

Summary

If you are going to successfully build your Business Case and Personal Case for partnership you will need to carve out time to learn new skills, go out and win your own work and take on new responsibilities. To create the time needed, you will need to identify ways in which you can become more productive by:

- Delegating more effectively
- Being more disciplined about what you will stop doing
- Learning to say "no"
- Stopping procrastination
- Having a default calendar
- Minimising your interruptions and distractions

Action Points

1. At the beginning of each week, ask yourself, *What are the 3 most important results that I must achieve this week that will make a difference to my Partner Track Plan and my team's performance?* Work out how you are going to achieve them and add these tasks to your Weekly Planner.

2. Start using your Weekly Planner.

3. Find an opportunity every day to practice your delegation skills.

4. If you struggle to say "no" to requests, have a go at gracefully declining the tasks or opportunities that come your way, which you should not be doing.

5. Use your firm's time recording system to review how much time you are spending on your key roles and responsibilities. Can you see a pattern emerging? Are you investing time on the things that will help and progress your Business Case and Personal Case?

6. Ask your Mentor and Sponsoring Partner how they found the time to build up their Business Case and Personal Case when they were on Partner Track?

7. Introduce a default diary into your calendar to make sure that you are integrating business development and team management activities into your day job.

8. Look at your Partner Track Plan Goals, Milestones and Objectives; i.e. your rocks. When can you plan these rocks into your diary?

Further resources

BOOKS

Use these books to help you become more productive and effective at work:

- *Eat That Frog!: Get More of the Important Things Done – Today!*, Brian Tracy, ISBN 978-1444765427

- *How to be a Productivity Ninja: Worry Less, Achieve More and Love What You Do*, Graham Allcott, ISBN 978-1848316836

- *The 7 Habits of Highly Effective People*, Stephen R. Covey, ISBN 978-0684858395

- *Assertiveness at Work: A Practical Guide to Handling Awkward Situations*, Ken Back and Kate Back, ISBN 978-007711428-2

- *Getting Things Done: How to Achieve Stress-free Productivity*, David Allen, ISBN 978-0749922641

- *Organizing from the Inside Out: the Foolproof System for Organizing Your Home, Your Office and Your Life*, Julie Morgenstern, ISBN 978-0805075892

WEBSITES

- Free time management plans and templates: http://www.howtomakepartner.com

- Dr Rob Rawson's blog – The Time Management expert: http://www.timemanagement.com/blog/

3

Making sure you have all the support you need

Topics covered in this chapter:

- The importance of your support team
- How to build a strong and positive relationship with your Sponsoring Partner
- How to use your Mentor to build your Business Case and Personal Case

When you run the marathon, you run against the distance, not against the other runners and not against the time.

HAILE GEBRSELASSIE

In the last two chapters we have been talking about how being on Partner Track is a marathon, not a sprint. Therefore, like any good long distance endurance athlete, you will need your own support team to help and support you along the way. Your support team is composed of people who are drawn from your personal, professional and family network. All the members of your support team have an important role to play in helping you achieve your aim of making partner and living to tell the tale. However, the two most important members of your support team whilst you are on Partner Track are your Mentor and your Sponsoring Partner.

This chapter provides the information that you need to build the right support team around you, in particular helping you leverage your relationship with your Mentor.

The importance of your support team

As I have mentioned before, being on Partner Track is like having two jobs. You can't successfully do two jobs in isolation. Your support team is there to help and guide you, take some of the strain, whilst keeping you fresh and energised for the journey ahead. They will be at your side throughout your journey on Partner Track.

Who should be in your support team?

Of course the exact make up of a support team will be different for everyone. However, an effective support team when you are on Partner Track is likely to have people playing five different types of roles.

Mentor: Your Mentor is someone in your firm who is more experienced, can act as a sounding board and provide objective guidance and feedback. When you are on Partner Track they play a vital role in helping you take the step up to partner. The right Mentor will:

- Help grow your profile within the partnership group, particularly in areas you have had little previous contact with

- Give you the insider knowledge on who you need to spend time with to strengthen your Personal Case

- Become one of your best advocates when the partners meet to discuss who should be made up to partner.

Sponsoring Partner: This person is normally the Head of your department or practice area. They are typically the person who will decide whether you are ready or not to go on Partner Track and be recommended for partnership. If you don't have their blessing to go for partnership then it will be pretty much nigh on impossible to make partner at your firm. You normally get no say in who will be your Sponsoring Partner. A Sponsoring Partner can act in a pretty similar role to your Mentor, for example help to grow your profile, be your best advocate, help you secure the coaching and personal development you need and give you the insider knowledge. In some firms your Sponsoring Partner is the person who will write and pitch your Business Case to the partners.

If you are aiming to get to partner as a lateral hire, it will be your Sponsoring Partner who will be the person championing your cause within the firm.

External Coach: There are many benefits to having your own executive or career coach who is independent from your firm, although your firm may be paying for their time. Your own coach helps you to take time out from the hurly-burly of your work life to focus on what really matters to you. They will also work with you in acquiring the key skills and knowledge required to make partner. It can be a very lonely time on Partner Track because you are not yet a partner, but no longer 'one of the team'. An independent coach can often be the only person you can totally confide in without fear of risking your progression to partner.

Family: Having a supportive and happy home life is important. It is very difficult to truly excel at work if you are having long-term problems with your family life.

Friends inside of work: By going for partner in your firm you are committing the next 5+ years of your life to this firm. Therefore, if you are going to be your best at work you need to have colleagues whom you like, trust, respect and think of as friends. If you find that you have very few friends at work, then this is a sign that you may need to seriously consider moving firms.

How to build a strong and positive relationship with your Sponsoring Partner

As your Sponsoring Partner is the person who recommends you for partnership, this is a crucial member of your support team. If this relationship has broken down or is weak your partnership ambitions may be effectively blocked at your firm.

Here are some tips to strengthen this core relationship:

Be aware of their personal agendas

Every partner in a firm is constantly juggling multiple agendas; their personal agenda, the firm's agenda, other partners' agendas and their team members' agendas. Not all of these agendas may be aligned! Therefore, you need to find out what is motivating them and what behind-the-scenes stress or dramas they may be managing in the background. The more you can align your agenda with what they want and need, the easier it will be to have their backing.

Communicate, communicate, communicate

Far too many professionals worry about being completely open and honest about their career aspirations and concerns with their Sponsoring Partner. Generally the more open you can be, the easier it is for your Sponsoring Partner to fully support you and help to remove the road blocks in your way. Aim to sit down with your Sponsoring Partner at least quarterly to have a chat about how the both of you think things are going. This doesn't need to be a long chat; 10 minutes may be all it takes.

Know how to manage them

Managing upwards is an important skill within a partnership. Make sure you know how they like to work, take decisions and receive information. Then ensure that you flex your style so that you communicate to them in their preferred style and give them information in a format that suits them.

Find ways to help them

Having a very supportive team member who you can rely on, just makes a team leader's life so much easier. Your aim is to see if you can become that team member for your Sponsoring Partner. How can you find small or big ways to help them?

How does a Mentor help you build your Business and Personal Case?

The right Mentor for you will become your secret weapon whilst you are on Partner Track. Of course, the right person will undertake the normal sort of roles that you can expect from any mentoring relationship, e.g.

- Critical friend, telling the mentee the uncomfortable truth that only a true friend can

- Sounding board, giving the mentee the chance to try out ideas and approaches in a safe environment

- Role model, providing an example from which the mentee can learn

- Coach, helping a mentee to acquire new skills and abilities

- Networker, helping a mentee develop the connections they need to gain experience, get a job, promotion and so on

- Facilitator, helping set and achieve objectives.

However, there are four key ways in which you can really leverage your relationship with your Mentor.

Help grow your profile within the partnership group, particularly in areas you have had little previous contact with

In an ideal world you would have been growing your profile across the firm from the early days of your career. However, you may be a senior lateral hire or just not socialised or worked with many of the partners outside of your own service line or sector team. This is where a mentor who is external to your practice area can help you to build your profile. Just by associating with them and being seen with them, your profile will grow outside of your own department; essential for when it comes to partnership vote time.

Give you the insider knowledge on who you need to spend time with to strengthen your Personal Case

Not everyone is created equal, and this is spot on when it comes to the partners in your firm. There are always going to be some partners that are more influential than others. Your Mentor can help you prioritise who you *must* have on your side and how to gain their trust, respect and advocacy.

Become one of your best advocates when the partners meet to discuss who should be made up to partner.

Most of the conversations about who is going to be ready for partnership takes place behind closed doors, either formally or informally between partners. The more advocates you have the more chance that you will be the person who gets partnership. One very strong influencer who is an advocate for you may be what you need to convince other partners that you are ready for partnership.

Share how they tackled the many challenges of being on Partner Track

As I've previously stated many times in this book, being on Partner Track is the hardest career transition you will do within the professions. Your Mentor will be a great source of pragmatic advice on how they coped, and the strategies they used to overcome the hurdles that face you. Because they have been in your position but also know what is really important for their fellow partners, they are ideally placed to help you prioritise where you should be spending your time. For example, the Mentor of one of my coaching clients was able to reassure her exactly what the rest of the partnership would want to see her doing to put her forward for partnership.

How to decide on who should be your Mentor

The best Mentor for you when you are on Partner Track will be someone who:

- Is external to your practice area
- Has the time to spend with you
- Is seen and known to be highly influential within the partnership
- You respect and like, and this feeling is mutual.

Case Study: Faye

Faye's firm had recently merged in the last 2 years. As a litigator she had strong relationships with people in her sector teams who sent her work. However, she wasn't widely known in the firm's core area of property or the partners from the other part of the merged firm. One of her personal development areas was to develop strong Referral Networks. As a result she chose a mentor from the firm's commercial property team who was known for being very good at developing Referral Networks. She did this for three reasons: it helped build her profile in property, she got to know partners from the other side of the merged firm, and she was able to learn how to create strong Referral Networks from someone who had been there and done that.

How to get the most from your Mentor

It is up to you to drive the relationship with your Mentor. To get the most out of this relationship:

- Set expectations from the outset of your relationship about what you both expect and want from each other
- Be honest with yourself and your Mentor, particularly if the relationship isn't progressing as you would like
- Prepare for your sessions with your Mentor and don't be afraid to have your own ideas and views
- Get dates diarised for your meetings in advance
- Do your action points from any meeting with your Mentor
- Agree with each other in what circumstances it is OK to postpone a meeting between the two of you.

Use the Career Kitbag's 'Guide to getting the most out of your relationship with your mentor' to help set up an effective relationship with your mentor. The guide includes a mentor/ mentee contract, which will help you set the right expectations between the two of you.

Summary

Having your own support team who help and cheer you along the way is vital if you are going to make it successfully through Partner Track to partner. The two most important members of your team are your Sponsoring Partner and your Mentor.

Your Sponsoring Partner is normally chosen for you and very often the head of your practice area. If you don't have a strong relationship with your Sponsoring Partner, then you are unlikely to make partner in your firm.

A good mentor will play many roles for you, but ultimately will be someone who you respect and like. They will become, alongside your Sponsoring Partner, your best advocate for you within the partnership group. Make sure you choose a mentor who is in a different practice area to you and has strengths or a skill set which you would like to gain.

Action Points

1. Identify an influential partner outside of your practice area who you have good rapport with, and ask them to be your Mentor. Make sure you present a case on what you want, what is motivating you to get to partner, and why you have chosen that person to be your Mentor.

2. Look for role models within and outside of your firm, who are recognised leaders in their field. Do some research to find out how they have achieved their success, what you can

learn from their experience, and how this can help your own career.

3. Look around you, who is in your support team? Who is missing from the team? What action could you take today to build stronger relationships between you and your support team?

4. Draw a diagram showing the members of your support team. Make a few notes under each name reminding you of what their strengths are in their support role.

5. Get into the habit of storing up examples and scenarios that you would appreciate guidance on to discuss with your Mentor.

Further Resources

Websites

- *How to make partner* includes articles on how to get the best out of your relationship with your Mentor: http://www.howtomakepartner.com

4

Keeping healthy for your journey on Partner Track

Topics covered in this chapter:

- The signs of stress and how to avoid burnout
- How to pace yourself to avoid becoming overwhelmed

❝ Life ain't no dress rehearsal.

BERNIE MAC

Being on Partner Track is a good sign that your long journey to make partner is coming to its concluding stages. However, you've just started the hardest part of your journey. This means you will need to stay healthy, both mentally and physically, to give yourself the optimum chance of making partner. Sadly many talented professionals never make it to partnership, because their body, and subsequent health, is unable to handle the lifestyle that the commitment to making partner so often demands.

This chapter gives your strategies to avoid burnout and becoming overwhelmed when you are on Partner Track.

The common signs of stress and how to avoid burnout

❝ Stress is still not something lawyers are comfortable talking about.

CATRIN MILLS[1]

---

1   *Effective Stress Management Techniques for Lawyers*, Catrin Mills, ISBN 978-1907787089

Common signs of stress include:

- Constantly feeling angry or getting angry easily
- Feeling down or depressed, often without knowing why
- Always feeling anxious, nervous, or constantly worried
- Either feeling hungry all the time, or having no appetite at all
- Feeling constantly overwhelmed
- Crying, or feeling like crying, a lot of the time
- Feeling constantly tired, and having trouble sleeping
- Not being able to concentrate
- Having to use alcohol or recreational drugs to be able to relax or wind down at the end of the day
- Poor skin; e.g. eczema, acne
- Hormonal swings or imbalances, particularly for females
- Digestive discomfort, for example irritable bowel syndrome and heartburn.

Note: If you find that you can personally relate to three or more of the signs on this list, then you need to seek professional advice and take action to reduce your stress levels.

 Use the Career Kitbag's Burnout Self-Assessment tool to see whether you are at risk of burning out

Everyone is different, and so the right amount of pressure for one person may be too high for another. Over time, people create coping strategies and mechanisms to be able to increase the level of pressure that they can deal with, while still maintaining peak performance and not suffering the side effects of unmanaged stress. It's when you either don't create these coping strategies and mechanisms – or when they become insufficient – that your health really starts to suffer from the effects of this unmanaged stress.

We are now going to look at what those coping strategies and mechanisms may be to reduce your stress levels and avoid burnout.

Increase your general level of activity

The human body was designed for physical activity – often walking 10km in a day to forage for food and get water. How many professionals would now be able to walk that distance every day?

Physical activity, as well as being a great stress reduction tool, is vital for our mental wellbeing and stamina. For example, just thirty minutes of brisk activity five days a week could significantly reduce your chances of having a heart attack. Let's now look in more detail how just a small shift in your level of activity helps your all-round general wellbeing and consequently enables you to maintain more periods of peak performance, regardless of the amount of pressure you are under at the time.

When you exercise, your body starts to produce serotonin. Serotonin enhances your mind and helps you clarify your thinking. This is why it often gets easier to take a decision, work out what's going on or cope with an event if you go for a walk or run. However, serotonin has even more benefits to our health. It is the precursor to melatonin, which is the chemical our body produces to help reach deep sleep. When you sleep deeply you wake up in the morning fully refreshed and ready to tackle the day. In turn, you've more energy left to do more exercise and therefore produce more serotonin, which makes you a happier and more effective person because you can think more clearly ... and so on, in a virtuous circle.

Exercise after work

Our bodies come hard-wired with the *fight or flight* response, which was meant to only be triggered once or twice a week. For example, when hunting for food or being under attack from a predator. In the *fight or flight* response, a series of complex hormonal changes occurs, which prepares our body to take emergency action. Adrenaline is produced – the equivalent of giving our body a shot of rocket fuel. The only way we can dissipate this rocket fuel is to either do some activity or proactively relax. Unreleased, adrenaline will accumulate in the body. Exercising after work becomes a great way of reducing the adrenaline in your body and it will help you to switch off your mind when it is time for sleep.

Take regular holidays

Taking a break from work can give your body much needed time to rest and recuperate. If you have got into a vicious cycle where you need to keep hitting the adrenaline button just to keep going, then taking annual leave may be the only way to break the cycle. You don't actually have to go away on holiday, just ensure that you are not working and focus on spending time recharging your mental and physical batteries.

Have a life outside of work

The book *How to make partner and still have a life*[2], talks about the importance of feeding your soul. This is the concept where you spend time outside work doing stuff you genuinely enjoy and socialise with people who make you feel good about yourself. Having a meaningful and enjoyable existence outside of work will increase your resilience to cope with the extreme pressure you will be under on Partner Track.

Eat healthily and avoid food containing high levels of processed sugar

Stress and nutrition have always been linked. Foods with high nutritional value can actively help you to reduce your stress levels. The opposite is also true; there are some foods and drinks which when consumed in moderation can increase your stress levels.

Food and drinks that have been proven to trigger and aggravate stress include:

- Foods containing caffeine, e.g. coffee, chocolate, tea and energy drinks

2 *How to Make Partner and Still Have a Life*, Jo Larbie and Heather Townsend, ISBN 978-0749466558

- Fast foods and takeaways
- Alcohol
- Fizzy and sugary soft drinks.

You may find you *need* your regular dose of caffeine to get through the day at work. However, it is worth noting that caffeine is a neuro-stimulator that heightens stress. Too much stress makes you anxious. Stimulation from caffeine can increase this anxiety and reduce the quality of your sleep.

After a long hard day at work many people find it so easy to pick up a curry on the way home from work. Takeaways and junk food normally contain high levels of protein, fats and carbohydrates and low levels of vital minerals and vitamins. This combination can induce stress.

Stress causes an increase in your blood sugar levels. Eating food with high levels of processed sugar can then significantly increase these levels. Prolonged periods of time with high blood sugar levels can be a contributory factor in the development of diabetes.

Lean on your support team

In Chapter 3 we talked about the importance of your support team. Your support team is there to help you during the good times and the bad times. A conversation with your Sponsoring Partner, Mentor or External Coach may be just what you need to lower your stress levels.

How to pace yourself to avoid becoming overwhelmed

With so much that you need to do on top of the day job it is easy to become stressed when you are on Partner Track. Here are some ways of pacing yourself to avoid becoming overwhelmed:

Accept that you are in a marathon not a sprint

If you haven't already broken up your Goals to make partner into realistic Milestones, as suggested in Chapter 1, then I encourage you to do so now. As the saying goes, a journey of a thousand miles starts with a single step. It is much easier to work towards smaller short-term Milestones than aim to do everything in one go.

Case Study: Simon

Simon was facing an uphill task. He needed to go from having zero clients of his own to building a client portfolio worth £800k. It seemed like an impossible Goal. So he worked with his Coach to break down the Goal into more easily achievable Milestones. He set himself monthly objectives and metrics for his business development activity levels. After he had done this and started working towards the much smaller Milestones and Objectives, he felt far more in control and confident that he could build a partner-sized client portfolio within 2 years.

Be realistic with your time

Everyone has 24 hours in a day. If you try and cram in too much to do in one day you will soon get disillusioned and potentially give up on your aim of making it to partner. Therefore, look through your diary each week. What is realistic to achieve on your Partner Track Plan this week?

Remember it is better to be the tortoise than the hare

Everyone is on a different career path. I know it is hard to see your peers accelerating their career ahead of yours. However, the right time to make it to partner will be the right time for you personally – not when the first people in your peer group make it. It is far better to take a little longer to get something rather than not get it at all by rushing. After all, not being ready for the role of partner when you get made up to it can be a very harmful career-limiting move.

Use a Partner Track Plan to pace yourself

It can be very tempting to try and do everything now. That is the quick way to burning out. Your Partner Track Plan will be an essential tool to keep yourself focused, but allow you to pace yourself on Partner Track.

 Use the Career Kitbag's Partner Track Plan to help you pace yourself and avoid burnout when you are on Partner Track.

Summary

Like any top athlete you need to make sure you are fit and healthy to successfully make the transition from senior associate/director to partner. This means you need to have created effective personal coping mechanisms and strategies to be able to handle the stress.

Commit to eating healthily and exercising regularly as a way of helping your body work at optimum levels of performance and reduce your stress levels.

Action Points

1. Look through the list of common signs of stress contained in this chapter. If you are regularly suffering from three or more of them then consult with a medical professional.

2. Consider your current workload and stress levels, and decide whether taking some annual leave might be sensible.

3. Get into the habit of switching your e-mail off when you finish work for the day.

4. If you are starting to feel overwhelmed then book some time in with someone you trust to talk through the causes of your high stress levels.

5. Start spending some of your weekly non-work time on something you enjoy that will help you to relax and unwind.

6. Plan to take a minimum of a 15-minute brisk walk or activity every day. Add this into your Weekly Planner. What opportunities do you have to do this activity with family and friends inside and outside of work?

7. Plan your meals for the next week so that you always have an easy, quick and nutritious meal after a long and tough day.

8. Ask your children, if you have them, what they would like to do with you regularly at weekends.

9. Get into the habit of having a regular date night with your partner or friends.

10. Find a form of exercise that you enjoy, such as swimming, yoga, pilates or running, and participate in this activity at least once a week. Make sure this goes into your Weekly Planner.

Further resources

BOOKS

Use these books to help explore more about building your resilience and reducing your stress levels:

- *Effective Stress Management Techniques for Lawyers*, Catrin Mills, ISBN 978-1907787089

- *Manage Yourself, Manage your Life: Vital NLP technique for personal well-being and professional success*, Ian McDermott and Ian Shircore, ISBN 978-0749919900

WEBSITES

- For more help on keeping your body working at peak performance contact Chris Williams at Momentum 4: http://www.momentum4.co.uk

- The Cognitus *destress at your desk blog* has a large amount of tips, techniques and strategies to help you reduce your stress levels at work: http://cognitusuk.com/blog/

PART II

Doing the research on yourself and your firm

In this part of the book, we will consider the research and due diligence you need to do before accepting an offer of partnership:

- Are you a good fit for partner?
- Are you right for your firm?
- What reputational or financial risk will you be taking on as a partner in your firm?
- How will your capital contribution be used?
- How will you get paid as a partner?
- What are you signing up to in your firm's Partnership Agreement?
- What liabilities are you taking on by becoming a partner?

5

Final check: Are you a good fit for partner?

Topics covered in this chapter:

- What changes when you transition from senior employee to owner of the business?

- Is partnership what you really want?

- Do you 'fit' in your firm?

For the past 33 years, I have looked in the mirror every morning and asked myself: 'If today were the last day of my life, would I want to do what I am about to do today?' And whenever the answer has been 'No' for too many days in a row, I know I need to change something.

STEVE JOBS

Up until now this book has not questioned your decision to make partner. However, before you commit a huge amount of time and effort to making it successfully through Partner Track, it is time to check what you really want for your career. Is it partnership in your firm, or in another firm? Or, to be blunt, have you just been seduced by the financial rewards and status that goes with making partner? Or have you been on the career treadmill and not been able to step off and really consider what you want for your future career? A few times I have worked with clients who thought that they have wanted to make partner at their firm. However, when they actually get close and can, so to speak, smell the coffee, they realise that partnership at their firm isn't for them.

This chapter explores what it really means to be a partner in your firm and whether you are a good fit for your firm.

What changes when you transition from senior employee to owner of the business?

Far too often I come across people who see making partner as just another promotion in their career. Going from senior fee earner to partner is not a promotion, it is the process where you stop being employed, start your life as a business owner, and become a real decision maker in your firm. The mindset shift from employee to employer is often the hardest part of the Partner Track process. For example, as a partner:

- Business development is not optional or something you only do when your client workload is low. Business development is part of the day job.

- Creating harmony and positive working relationships within the partner group is often more important than being right.

- You need to motivate your whole team or practice area rather than just yourself

- It is no longer just about hitting your billable time targets, it is making sure that anything you do is focused on helping the firm increase its profitable revenue

- You share in the profits rather than get paid a salary. This means that if the firm is having a lean year, you may be required to put your own money into the firm and forego your 'salary'.

- There will be times that you will have to take decisions which will not be universally popular. For example, performance managing someone who you trained with and consider a good friend.

- The short- and long-term health of the firm and how it is led and managed is now your responsibility.

Is partnership what you really want?

Making partner is not the only destination for your career. Success shouldn't be defined by your job title, but by how fulfilled and happy you are, inside and outside of work.

Is becoming a partner playing to your strengths?

Before you carry on reading this book take a moment to stop and reflect. Do your expectations of what it means to be a partner match up with the realities of the partner role? Are you a good fit for partner? The best decision for you and your future career is one where you are fulfilled and happy doing what you do. You are not failing if you decide to not go for partner.

The advantages of making partner

Having *Partner* on your business card brings a level of professional respect and status. In some ways it is also a validation of your professional worth and merit. With that professional respect normally come the rewards of owning a slice of the firm. Of course in the years when profits are low, there is no certainty as a junior partner that you will earn more than the director/senior associates in your firm. It is probably fair to say that as a partner in a large, Big 4 or Magic Circle firm, your drawings (i.e. share of the firm's profits) will be substantial.

One of the benefits of being a partner is you have a little more freedom to organise how you want to run your life. After all, if you achieve your targets it doesn't matter whether you take 35 days holiday a year or 5 days holiday a year. It also doesn't matter whether you decide to work from home one day a week. Very often the only thing holding you back, as a partner, from taking a bit of 'life' back from your firm, is your own routine and way of working.

When you own a slice of the firm, you have the luxury of building your part of the practice around what you want (well, within reason). This means you can delegate down the stuff you don't like and just focus on what you enjoy and are good at. In many ways this is similar to the advantages of running a small business, but with a much bigger support structure around you.

The disadvantages of making partner

Let's strip away the glitz and glamour of being partner and actually look at what you need to do to get there. The years when you are on Partner Track and get to be a junior partner are probably some of the hardest you will ever work. Hitting high billable targets *and* growing your own profile and client portfolio is tough work. You will be required to work outside of the 8–6 working day and attend events in your own time to 'get your name out there'.

Not everyone is cut out to make partner. After all, it takes a multi-talented professional to do the three roles all partners need to do well: Business Winner, Client Relationship Manager and Team Leader. If any one of these three things is really not what you want to do long term then you will struggle to really excel as a partner in not just your firm but in any professional practice.

Many firms, particularly the Big 4, Magic Circle and top global consulting firms demand a huge personal and long-term commitment from their partners. This isn't just a commitment to build and service a large client portfolio. It is to stay within the firm and do what it takes to help the firm run profitably. This could take the form of being relocated away from friends and family for the good of the firm.

Case Study: Matt

A PwC US Partner, Matt, on making it to partner, found himself relocating his family to Switzerland for a 3-year assignment in order to build up his international network. Whilst the assignment may sound glamorous, it came with a massive cost to family life. His children had to adapt to a new school system and rapidly learn a new language. Leaving her friends and family behind in the US made life in Switzerland for his wife. For a while this placed a massive strain on Matt's family life.

For example, when you become an equity partner you become self-employed and own a small slice of your firm. This means that the buck stops with you. At times this amount of responsibility can be incredibly stressful. For example, in your capacity as partner, you could be asked to:

- Be bound by a Partnership Vote that you don't necessary agree with

- Contribute a large chunk of capital into the firm when it needs additional funding

- Continually bring in profitable new client work

- Take decisions that could negatively affect people you care about in your firm.

Do you 'fit' in your firm?

By committing yourself to your firm as a partner you also commit to working with your current colleagues for many years. If you are to truly excel as a partner you need to feel that you fit into your firm. For example:

- Do you have good friends within your firm?

- Are you proud to work and represent your firm?

- Do you find that the firm's official and unofficial values are closely aligned with your own?

- Do you find yourself effortlessly fitting in with your firm?

- Do you have a sense of 'belonging' within your firm?

- Are you looking forward to the opportunity to collaborate with your partners for the good of the firm?

- Are you happy with what you will need to commit to the firm in order to get to partner?

If you answer *no* to any of these questions, then you need to take a long hard look at whether you are right for partnership in your current firm. Remember there are plenty more firms out there who may be a perfect fit for you.

Case Study: Lindsey

Lindsey was on track to make partner in her firm. However, when she found out she was pregnant her partners gave her an ultimatum. Either come back after her maternity leave on a full-time basis, as a client-facing fee earner and carry on to partner, or switch into a professional support lawyer role on a part-time basis. Neither option felt right to her. As a result she found a new role in a smaller law firm who were able to offer her a client-facing part-time role.

Summary

Before you spend hours working on your Business Case and Personal Case take the time to fully explore the implications of making partner in your firm. Then answer these questions: *Is this right for you?* and *Is it what you really want?* Or would you be better off making partner in another firm or even changing your career path altogether?

Action Points

1. Ask yourself if going for partnership is the right decision for you in your career.

2. Ask yourself whether you are really enjoying what you do now in your current role. Will this change be for the better or worse if you make partner. If you are not enjoying your career in the professions, then work with a career coach/counsellor to help you find the right career path for you.

Further resources

BOOKS

These books will help you check that you are making the right career decision to go for partner:

- *How to Make Partner and Still Have a Life*, Jo Larbie and Heather Townsend, ISBN 978-0749466558

- *Managing Transitions: Making the Most of Change*, William Bridges, ISBN 978-1857885415

- *More To Life Than Shoes: How to Kick-start Your Career and Change Your Life*, Nadia Finer and Emily Nash, ISBN 978-1848502505

- *Go to Work on Your Career*, Andy Gilbert and Nicky Frisby, ISBN 978-0953728442

WEBSITES

- Career Shifters Blog contains great advice for people who want to change their career: http://www.careershifters.org/blog

6

Doing due diligence on your firm

Topics covered in this chapter:

- Why you need to do your due diligence
- What due diligence you will need to do on your firm
- How much capital will you need to buy into your partnership
- What you will get paid as a partner
- Who should you consult to do your due diligence

It takes many good deeds to build a good reputation, and only one bad one to lose it.

BENJAMIN FRANKLIN

The last chapter explored whether you are a good fit for partnership and a good fit in your firm. In this chapter we will look at the due diligence you will need to do on your firm, and why doing your due diligence is essential.

Note: This chapter touches briefly on the tax and financial implications of becoming a partner in the UK. These may not be the same for people based in countries outside of the UK. Before you take any decision based on what you read in this book you are strongly advised to seek your own professional advice.

Why you need to do your due diligence

On the day you are admitted to the partnership you will:

- Resign and become self-employed
- Make a significant capital contribution to your firm

- Leave the firm's pension scheme
- Lose your employment rights
- Tie your personal reputation to the firm's reputation
- Stop receiving the benefits you were entitled to as an employee of your firm.

That's all on a 'promise' that you will be receiving significantly higher financial rewards and greater influence on your career and firm than you do now. Yes, none of these rewards are actually guaranteed. Given these slightly unpalatable facts and the impact on you if partnership doesn't work out, it is essential that you do your due diligence to protect your future reputation and financial investment.

How are most partnerships structured?

Most partnerships have now moved to being a limited liability partnership (LLP). An LLP is a partnership in which some or all of the partners (depending on the country they are based in) have limited liabilities. This means that in an LLP, one partner is not responsible or liable for another partner's misconduct or negligence. Therefore, unless a partner is personally involved in the negligence or malpractice, their personal assets would be sheltered. However, this doesn't mean you are immune from any wrongdoings of your partners. The LLP as well as the traditional partnership structure continues to be liable for the negligence of any of its partners, so the assets of the partnership remain at risk.

Some partnerships – often the more traditional 'old-school' firms – have not converted to an LLP structure. This means that the partners are all liable for the debts and obligations of the firm. As well as this, each partner is responsible for the liabilities of the other partners, and potentially the full amount of all the partnership liabilities.

Changes to the way partners in LLPs are taxed in the UK

When you become a member of the LLP you are taxed as if you are self-employed; i.e. moving from being taxed under Schedule E to

Schedule D. This means that your firm benefits from not having to pay National Insurance (NI) Contributions on the members' salaries and benefits in kind, such as private medical insurance. As a result, many firms – not just from the professions – converted to the LLP status to reduce their NI costs.

In 2014 in the UK, the government closed this tax loophole. Members of the LLP, for whom HMRC (the entity in the UK which collects taxes on behalf of the government) consider as not true partners, but 'salaried', are now classed for tax purposes as employed. This change in the tax rules in the UK has forced many firms to insist that all partners become equity partners. Another knock-on effect of the new tax rules in the UK, has been to force firms to prescribe a minimum capital stake or 'buy-in' amount for new equity partners. A member is at risk of being viewed as a 'salaried member' if their capital stake in the business is less than 25% of their annual drawings.

What due diligence do I need to do on my firm before accepting an offer of partnership?

What are you actually being offered?

The first thing you need to understand is what you are being offered. Are you being offered a salaried, equity or fixed-share partner role? Are you being offered a salaried role for a few years until you prove yourself and then will be offered equity? Similar to the traditional partnership model, LLPs can have several classes of members: equity and fixed-share equity members.

Salaried partner

The salaried partner role still does exist within an LLP. Salaried partners are still employees of the LLP, taxed as if they are employed, and not liable if their partnership runs into problems. The salaried partner role in a traditional partnership is a risky place to be. There is the authority that comes with having partner on the business card, but full liability for any wrongdoing by the partners in the firm. However this class of partner has no right to share in the profits of the firm. Very often salaried partners, regardless of the partnership legal structure, enjoy a bonus, over and above their annual salary, based on the firm's performance.

Fixed-share equity partner

Fixed-share equity partners, tend to be, but not always, the firm's junior partners. If you are offered partnership it is likely that you will be initially be offered a fixed-share partner role. Typically fixed-share partners are given a small slice of equity and sometimes guaranteed minimum drawings. However, this isn't always the case. Very often, newly admitted fixed-share equity partners come in at the bottom of a firm's profit-sharing model.

Full equity partner

The terms 'full equity' and 'fixed-share equity' partner refer to how partners are remunerated, and typically their seniority and voting rights with the practice. New partners will typically join the firm as a fixed-share equity partner and then progress through the ranks, particularly if the firm operates a 'lockstep' partner model, until they become a full equity partner. Full equity partners have typically demonstrated their ability to grow a profitable and sustainable client portfolio.

What are you signing up to in your Partnership Agreement?

Each partnership has a different Partnership Agreement. The Partnership Agreement is how the partners agree to run the business. It sets out:

- How the firm will be governed
- What the decision-making process is for important issues

- What issues will require a Partnership Vote before they can be officially ratified

- The role of the firm's Management Board

- How partners will be compensated which includes how profits will be distributed to the partners

- When drawings are paid

- General duties and expectations of a partner

- Capital contributions required by partners

- Who is responsible for the day-to-day financial management of the firm and control of expenses

- How firm expenses are split across the firm

- The firm's policies on parental leaves and sabbaticals

- What happens when partners exit the firm and timescales for partner's capital to be repaid to them

- Restrictive covenants placed on partners who leave the firm, whether willingly or otherwise.

Firm Governance

Different firms tend to govern themselves in different ways. The very largest firms are governed in a manner more akin to a large multinational business. The smallest firms can have all their partners involved in day-to-day management of the firm.

When you look through your Partnership Agreement you need to establish:

- What you will have authority over in your role as partner

- How the firm is actually governed and in particular the role of your firm's Management Board

- How the firm's Management Board is appointed or elected

- What partnership committees the firm has and their roles; e.g. the Partner Compensation Committee

- If your firm has a Partnership Council, what their role is, and how this will impact you personally.

Decision making in your firm

Professional Services firms are not known for their quick decision-making. The Partnership Agreement will set out what actually constitutes an important issue and the decision-making process for important issues. A Partnership Vote will be required for the most fundamental decisions, such as a firm merger, large capital expenditure projects, opening a new office, changing the compensation arrangements for partners, amending the Partnership Agreement or changing the firm name. Not every partner's vote is created equal. It is not unusual for full equity partners to have a higher weighted vote than a junior fixed-share equity partner.

Sometimes in the small firms every partner will need to be consulted on even the smallest decisions the firm will need to take. In most firms, the Management Board will make decisions about the day-to-day operation of the firm. The Board will sometimes include non-partners who have been brought into the firm for their specialist knowledge.

When you look through your Partnership Agreement you need to establish:

- What decisions within the firm you are entitled to be consulted on
- What decisions will need to go to a Partnership Vote
- How much your vote is actually worth compared to others in the partnership.

Partner profit allocation and partner compensation

You are going to be committing your long-term future to a firm. It is therefore essential that you have a thorough understanding of how your firm compensates its partners and allocates its profits through to the partners. You may find that your firm highly rewards its most senior partners regardless of what they actually contribute to the firm. Are you prepared to work exceptionally hard for a number of years for not much more reward than when you were an employee? Whilst this may not be fair, it may be what you are being asked to sign up to.

It is important to understand how you will be recognised for any non-billable related activity that you will be asked to do on behalf of the firm. For example, it is not unusual for junior partners in a practice area to be asked to take on a managerial responsibility such as the HR or Training partner role. In the more mature firms, partners' performance, and subsequent profit share, will be assessed on both billable and non-billable performance. This could include work-in-progress (WIP) and Lockup, debtor days, business development and contributing to the management and leadership of the firm.

Most partnership compensation schemes are influenced by the work that a partner brings into the firm. You will need to understand how you will be credited for:

- Client work you refer into the firm but don't service within your team

- Client work you service in your team which has been referred to you by another partner within the practice

- Client work you have helped win as part of a team of partners, which is serviced by your team and other fee earners across the practice.

For example, some firms do not credit non-partners when they bring work into the firm. Or worse still, partners in some firms have been known to take the credit for when their team members bring in work to the firm.

The Partnership Agreement will probably define when partners' drawings are paid. These are often paid out based on projected profits, with the balance of profits being paid out after the annual financial statements are prepared. If your firm is well-capitalised with a healthy and predictable cash flow, it may be in a position to distribute monthly drawings based on work-in-progress which hasn't yet been invoiced and paid. In smaller firms, or firms without the cash resources to distribute monthly drawings, the timings of drawings being allocated may be heavily influenced by the firm's cash flow and available working capital.

When you look through your Partnership Agreement you need to establish:

- How profits are distributed across the firm and what your share will be in the first few years
- How you will be recognised for non-billable activities and responsibilities
- How you are credited when you bring in work to the firm and work on other partners' client work
- Who decides the partnership compensation and how do they decide?
- Whether your firm publishes a table of how each of the partners are compensated
- If the firm's Partnership Agreement is flexible enough to cope with an extraordinary year
- When are drawings paid out and in what circumstances?

How your performance will be assessed

The Partnership Agreement is likely to set out the general duties of a partner, but it is unlikely to specify the performance criteria expected of a partner. The performance criteria will probably be documented in a different document or policy. If your firm distributes profits with a system that is based on performance, then you are likely to be given performance targets to achieve. Your compensation will then be linked to how well you have achieved your performance targets.

When you look through your Partnership Agreement you will need to establish:

- How your performance will be measured
- When your performance will be measured and by whom
- If or how your performance is linked to your share of the firm's profits
- What happens if you don't achieve your performance targets.

Capital contributions

As mentioned earlier in this chapter you will be requested to invest some capital into your firm when you become a partner. It is important that you fully understand how your capital will be used. The last thing that you want is to find out that your capital has been used to give an unsustainable business model a few extra months of life before it falls over. If your partnership is wound up, the partnership liabilities are paid first, and then any remaining assets distributed to the partners. However, there are unlikely to be any remaining assets to distribute as most firm's value is in their client list. You can expect any goodwill to disappear very quickly when a client finds that their professional advisor is in financial difficulty.

In the Partnership Agreement it will set out when you may be asked to contribute capital and also what happens when you exit. You will need to be absolutely clear what will happen to your capital when you exit the firm. In an ideal world the contents of your Capital Account and Drawings/Current Account will be paid to you in full promptly after leaving the firm. This isn't always the case. For example, if the firm has laid off a large tranche of partners it may not be able to afford to repay every partners' capital promptly. If you make a lateral move to a new firm and your old firm is slow to repay your capital it could prevent you from accessing a new line of credit to buy into your new firm.

When you look through your Partnership Agreement you will need to establish:

- How quickly do you get your capital back if you leave?
- Do you get your capital back in full when you leave?
- What your capital is being used for.

Overheads and liabilities

When you sign up as a partner you will take on several long-term liabilities. It is very important that you fully understand what these are. Liabilities could include professional liability, lease costs and bank debts. Whilst if you are a member of the LLP you are not liable for other partners' wrong-doings you still may find that the bank requires you to provide a personal guarantee for the partnership's borrowings. These borrowings could be to finance the purchase of premises or an overdraft for the firm.

Most firms have an element of skeletons in the closet, which could be potential Professional Indemnity (PI) claims or unresolved PI claims. These skeletons may come back to haunt you as equity partners are expected to share in both the pain and the gain of the firm. You may be able to negotiate a warranty or indemnity when you join the partnership against some of the known potential or unresolved PI claims that your firm may be carrying.

When you look through your Partnership Agreement you will need to establish:

- What exactly you are liable for
- What personal guarantees you will be required to sign
- What 'baggage' the firm has, which you would become liable for as an equity partner.

Flexible working provision

When you become self-employed you normally lose all of your employment rights, including as an example paid maternity leave. Whilst you may not be thinking about flexible working right now, it is worth seeing how your firm would handle any of their partners wanting to work part-time, work odd hours or take a sabbatical.

Exiting your firm

I'm guessing that the last thing you are thinking about at the moment is exiting your firm. However, you need to consider this before you sign up to anything that becomes untenable. Within the Partnership Agreement you need to find the notice period and what restrictive covenants you will have placed upon you if you leave the firm. This could be that you need to give the firm 12-months notice when you resign from the partnership. It is not unheard of for firms to ask their resigning partners – particularly if they are going to a competitor – to go on full-paid leave for the full 12-months. Partnership Agreements will also have a clause that stops you poaching the firm's clients for a 6-month+ period after you leave.

How to assess if your firm is solvent

As mentioned earlier, there is a very real and present danger that your capital contribution could be used to prop up an ailing firm. As well as risking your own money in this situation, and leaving you with hefty personal debts, you could also face a large reputational risk. Being a partner in a firm which goes bankrupt, is often seen to be a large black mark on your own reputation and character.

To get an idea of how solvent your firm is you need to have sight of, ideally, the last three years of annual accounts and the most up-to-date management accounts the firm has. After all, annual accounts can be massively out of date and, therefore, hide any growing financial hole the firm has.

The firm's balance sheet gives you a snapshot of your firm's assets and liabilities at a fixed point in time. The first test for the firm's solvency is to check that the firm's current assets are larger than its current liabilities. The next check you should do with the balance sheet is to look at the level of its working capital. The working capital of a firm can be worked out by taking the current assets (not the fixed assets) minus the current liabilities. If this is low or negative, then your firm may have cash flow problems.

Other areas to check include:

- High borrowings relative to the firm's share capital and reserves
- Negative cash flow or persistent long-term cash flow problems
- Debtors rising faster than turnover
- Large amounts of working capital tied up in work-in-progress
- High levels of written-off bad debts
- Net current liabilities where the firm has short-term debts greater than its readily realisable assets

- The current levels of partners' drawings are sustainable.

If you are concerned about anything financially related then do talk with the Finance Director in your firm, and get an independent accountant to review the accounts for you.

How to check that your firm is robust

As Arthur Andersen found out, it can only take one event to radically bring about the end of a professional services firm. The LLP firm structure was created partly in response to the overnight demise of Andersen. Of course, you don't have a crystal ball to identify what could go wrong whilst you are a partner. What you can do is understand how robust your firm actually is. For example:

- Look at the firm's PI insurance and claims track record. Above average or escalating PI costs could indicate that there is something very wrong with the firm and how it is managed. Additionally, look to see if there are any outstanding or potential PI claims that the firm is aware of.

- What are the 3-year trends in the firm's performance? If the trends carry on for the next few years will the firm still be profitable and solvent?

- Find out how reliant the firm is on its top 5–10% clients. How many of these clients could leave before the firm would be unprofitable?

- How dependent is the firm on its top work-winners? Would the firm struggle to bring in revenue if a few of them left, or a practice team upped and left?

- How prepared is your firm to take quick tough decisions when the market or economy turns against them? Many a firm has gone under because its partners refused to take action believing the problem would go away.

- How actively does the firm manage risk? What are the key risks that the firm is facing at the moment? Does it have a plan to mitigate these risks?

How well led and managed is your firm?

So far we have looked at the financial performance of the firm, and the importance of the contents of the Partnership Agreement. The final part of your due diligence is to look at how well led and managed your firm is. It is not uncommon for partnerships to be well managed but badly led, or vice versa. Bad leadership decisions such as stalling on a highly beneficial merger or delaying taking crucial decisions could drastically impact the profitability and sustainability of a firm. Therefore, it is worth finding out:

- What is the strategic plan for the firm and why is the firm's leadership following that particular strategy? Can you support this strategy?

- What are the firm's core values and culture? Is this something that you can role model both internally and externally?

- Does the firm have a clear idea of how current and future changes in their marketplace will impact it and a strong vision as to how to deal with this?

- Is there a culture of robust leadership in the firm with well-defined strategy as to how the firm will develop in the future with the management having the authority to implement the actions necessary to achieve this?

- To what extent will you, as a partner, be able to participate in/affect decisions concerning the future of the firm?

- Does the firm have a clear strategy and business plan for client and business development?

- How will you be involved in delivering this business development strategy?

- What support does your firm's marketing and business development team offer to new partners?

 Use the Career Kitbag's Due Diligence checklist to help you do all the essential due diligence checks to minimise any financial or reputational risk you will be entering into by joining the partnership.

Who should you consult to do your due diligence?

To give yourself as complete a picture as possible, you should make time to talk to the following people in your firm, and seek their views and opinions:

- The Finance Director (or equivalent)
- The HR Director (or equivalent)
- The Business Development Director (or equivalent)
- Your Head of department, Mentor, Sponsoring Partner and other partners and peers in your firm
- Decision makers from the firm's key clients
- The firm's marketing department
- Others in your personal support team

How much capital will you need to buy into a partnership

As a new partner and a new owner of the firm you will normally be required to buy a stake in your firm. It is often referred to as 'buying into your firm'. Your initial contribution could be as little as £5,000 or as much as £500,000+. For example, it would not be unusual for you to be expected to stump up capital between £30,000 and £100,000 for a Top 100 UK Law or Top 50 UK Accountancy Firm.

The amount of capital you will be asked to invest depends on:

- The size of your firm
- How well capitalised your firm is
- The equity stake you are being offered
- Your projected drawings as a junior partner
- The market value of your firm.

Ownership may be offered in a few different ways:

- Equal ownership, where all the partners own a similar amount of shares in the firm.

- Partial ownership, where you will become a minority owner in the business. This is often the case for new partners who don't yet have the financial means to buy into a larger stake in the partnership.

- Incremental ownership, where as your financial means increase you are able to buy into more of the firm. Very often your share of the profits is reinvested in the firm to allow you to increase your stake in the firm.

Your capital contribution normally buys an equity stake in the firm and a contribution to the firm's working capital. For small practices that own their premises, buying into these is often dealt with separately. To find out how much you need to buy in for the equity stake and working capital look at the partner's capital accounts on the balance sheet. This shows you how much the partners have contributed to the practice over time. Another way of identifying how much you will be required to buy in to a firm is to consider that under the tax rules in the UK, partners need to have a capital stake in their firm which is at least 25% of their annual drawings.

You may find that if you are a lateral hire to a partnership, and have a particularly valuable skill set or network of introducers, you may be offered a very good deal to join and buy into the partnership.

What does your capital contribution get used for?

Your capital contribution can be used in many ways; for example:

- Increase the firm's working capital
- Help the firm to pay out an exiting partner's capital in the firm
- Replace the firm's need to seek out other sources of funding
- Boost other partners' drawings.

Given the fact that most professional service firms have a one- to six-month time delay before the work completed is billed and paid, most firms have a significant sum of money tied up in work-in-progress. This means that your capital contribution is normally used to help improve the firm's working capital and offset the money tied up in work-in-progress. Part of your due diligence involves asking exactly how your firm will use your capital contribution.

How to raise the funds to buy into your firm

There are generally two routes to raising the funds to buy in to your firm. This is either by raising the finance through a bank loan or by 'under drawing' on your share of the firm's profits. Your own firm will have a preferred route to how they will allow you to raise the funds to buy your equity stake. However, most firms prefer their new partners to finance their capital stake by their own resources. Many firms will have arranged banking facilities to enable their partners to take out a partnership loan.

How will you get paid as a partner?

Partners are paid from the profits that the firm makes. This means that equity partners no longer receive a salary or a guaranteed fixed amount of money they will earn each year.

Each partner will have two accounts, a Capital Account and a Drawings/Current Account. The Partnership Agreement will determine how profits get distributed to the partners.

Capital Account

This is your account where your equity stake in the partnership is held. This account will include:

- Your initial and subsequent capital contributions to the partnership, which could be in the form of cash or the market value of other types of assets

- Any profits and losses earned by the business and allocated to you based on what is set out in the Partnership Agreement

- Distributions to the partners, such as the payment of a dividend or capital gain.

Drawings/Current Account

This is your account where you 'draw' down funds from your Capital Account in order to release funds to you personally. The best analogy is to consider that your drawings become the way you are now remunerated as a partner.

Profit Per Equity Partner (PEP)

Many firms publish their Profits Per Equity Partner figures. If your firm is an LLP, it is fairly easy to work out, from annual published year-end accounts, what the average PEP for your firm is. However, this PEP figure is not what you will receive in your first few years as a partner. In fact, you may never achieve the publicly stated PEP figure for your partnership. The wider the PEP spread, the harder it will be to achieve a personal profit share greater than the PEP for your partnership. Be aware that if there is a very large spread then your initial capital contribution may actually be going towards lining the pockets of the top earners in the partnership, rather than the actual working capital of the partnership.

Different profit distribution policies

The way that each firm distributes profits to its partners is set out in its Partnership Agreement. Every firm has a different way of doing it! However, most firms tend to adopt aspects of these four models:

Lockstep: This is a model where partners get paid based on their seniority rather than what the partner brings into the firm. New partners will join their partnership with a certain number of 'points'. They will accrue new points over time based on their performance and/or tenure in the role. Over time they will reach a set maximum number of points and full equity partner status. Some firms will have a policy where points can be deducted for poor performance. Clifford Chance LLP uses this model to distribute profits to its members.

Extract from *Clifford Chance LLP Annual Review 2014*[3]:

Partnership remuneration is transparent to the partnership. Equity partners are paid a proportion of the firm's global profits according to their position on the lockstep. As our equity partners are the owners of the firm as well as executives, their compensation reflects their shareholder dividend as well as pay. Equity partners do not receive options or incentives of any sort and no equity partner has guaranteed earnings.

'Eat everything you kill' or *'Source of origination'*: This is a model where each partner earns only what they have generated in income, after covering their share of the firm's expenses and wage bill. Very often this model is adapted so that each partner receives a share of the partnership profits up to a certain amount. The remaining profits are distributed to the partner who 'originated' the work. An 'eat everything you kill' model acts as an incentive for partners to go out and win work. However as some firms have found[4], this can lead to poor behaviour by partners who don't want to introduce their clients to other partners for fear of losing the credit for the client's fees.

Performance-related pay: This is where partners are allocated a share of their drawings based on the results they achieved in the year. It is similar to the 'eat everything you kill' model but takes into account billable and non-billable performance.

Equal profit-sharing amongst partners: This is where, regardless of seniority or status, profits are shared equally amongst the firm's partners. This model tends to be used by only the smallest firms.

---

3 http://www.cliffordchance.com/content/dam/cliffordchance/About_us/Corpo-rate_Responsibility/CC%20Annual%20Review%202014.pdf

4 http://www.newrepublic.com/article/113941/big-law-firms-trouble-when-money-dries

Drawings in your first year

Every firm takes a very different approach to the drawings you will be able to make in your first year. For example, here is the policy for partners' drawings in BDO as set out in their *Report to the members for the 52 weeks ended 4 July 2014*[5]:

The policy for members' drawings is to distribute the majority of profit during the financial period, taking into account the need to retain sufficient funds to settle members' income tax liabilities and to finance the working capital and other needs of the business. The Leadership Team sets the level of members' monthly drawings and reviews this at least annually.

The drawings you receive in your first few years will be typically:

Drawings = (your share of the partnership profits) - (interest and capital repayments on any partnership loan) - (income tax) - (capital contributions to the firm)

You may find that in your first few years as an equity partner, particularly if your firm is having some lean years, that you will receive less in drawings than when you were employed by the firm.

Before you commit to becoming a partner you need to find out the level of income you can expect as a junior partner in your practice. The best way to find out how you will be compensated in your first few years as a partner is to request copies of the annual reports for the last three years and a copy of the Partnership Agreement, particularly the policy on partner remuneration. This will give you an idea of how much your share of the drawings will be as a junior partner.

Summary

Becoming a partner in a firm means you will need to make a large investment in a firm and tie your personal reputation to the firm's fortunes. To protect your financial investment and personal reputation

5   http://www.bdo.co.uk/__data/assets/pdf_file/0004/1051267/7615-Report-to-members-2014FINAL.pdf

you need to complete your own due diligence on your firm. Your due diligence exercise should involve partners in the firm, outside specialists and heads of the firm's practice management departments.

Action Points

1. Find out when you are able to review your Partnership Agreement. Get your Partnership Agreement reviewed by an external expert to identify exactly what you are signing up to as a partner in your firm.

2. Identify what your likely drawings will be as a junior partner and how your firm distributes its profits amongst its members.

3. Book time with your firm's Head of Finance to determine the likely capital contribution you will be asked to make to join the partnership. Find out how your capital contribution will be used by the firm. In your discussion identify if there are any planned capital expenditures in the next few years that partners will be asked to contribute to.

4. Identify what you are actually being offered by your partners. Salaried partner? Fixed-share equity partner? Full equity partner?

5. Discover how to progress from being a junior partner through to a full equity partner in your firm. What will you be expected to achieve, do or demonstrate?

6. Discern how your firm makes decisions within the partnership group. What decisions will you have a say in as a partner? What responsibilities do partners delegate to the Management Board?

7. Book time in with some recently appointed partners in your firm. How did they find their transition from employee to partner? How is their performance assessed now? What do they wish someone had told them in hindsight?

8. Ask for details of any PI claims your firm has made in the last 3 years and whether there are any unresolved PI claims in the

pipeline. Identify what other liabilities, personal guarantees or overheads you will become liable for when you become a partner.

9. Obtain up-to-date financial records for your firm, including recent management accounts, and get an accountant to review them for you. Ask your accountant to give you an honest opinion of how solvent your firm is and the level of risk you would be taking on by being an equity partner.

10. Understand the implications to you and your investment in the firm if you decide to exit the partnership. What restrictive covenants will you be subjected to?

11. Do your research to find out how robust the firm is.

12. Request copies of the firm's future plans. Ask yourself, is this something I want to be a part of?

Further resources

BOOKS

This book will help you read financial reports:

- *FT Guide to Finance for Non Financial Managers: The Numbers Game and How to Win It*, Jo Haigh, ISBN 978-0273756200

Creating a persuasive Business Case for partnership

Your Business Case for Partnership is where you demonstrate the commercial advantage to your partners of admitting you to the partnership.

In this part of the book, we consider exactly what you need to do to create and then articulate your Business Case to your partners. For example:

- What is your Business Case?
- How to demonstrate your Business Case if you are in industry or a non-fee earner
- How to become the Go-To Expert
- How to build Referral Networks

7

Building your Business Case

Topics covered in this chapter:

- What is your Business Case?
- Common mistakes people make with their Business Case
- How to build your Business Case if you are currently in industry
- The commercial realities of inheriting a partner's portfolio

If one does not know to which port one is sailing, no wind is favourable.

LUCIUS ANNAEUS SENECA

What is your Business Case?

Before the partnership can admit any new partner they need to have a business case for doing so. Your Business Case is where you demonstrate the commercial advantage for your partners to make you up to partner. A Business Case will typically be built on one of the following premises:

- A partner is retiring and the department needs a replacement partner
- A part of the firm is growing and needs another partner-level person to help service this part of the business
- You have personally built a profitable partner-sized client portfolio, which your partnership cannot afford to lose
- You have a great network of trusted contacts which you can use to open doors for other partners in the firm

- You have strong relationships within, and deep knowledge of one particular client that your firm would like to increase its business with

- There is an opportunity to enter a new marketplace or offer a new service stream that you can build into a profitable client portfolio, which in turn will justify your admission into the partnership. You also need *Partner* on your business card to build this new revenue stream for your firm.

Any well-organised partnership will be identifying where there is a Business Case for a new partner many years in advance. They will then work with a selection of candidates to build a Personal Case for partnership. This then gives the partnership choices about who will be the best candidate for the new partner role.

How does your Business Case differ from your Personal Case?

Very often your Personal Case for partnership is lumped together in your Business Case for partnership. Your Personal Case is where you show that you meet the criteria for partnership and your partners like and trust you enough to make you up to partner. Your Business Case is where you demonstrate the *commercial* advantage as to why the partnership needs a new partner. When you hear partners in your firm talk about your Business Case, do query whether they really mean just your Business Case or your *Business Case and Personal Case*.

What do you need to show in your Business Case?

It depends! Every firm is different in its process for admitting new partners into the partnership. This means the way you need to construct and evidence your Business Case will be different depending on the firm you are in. Demonstrating your Business Case for partnership could be anything from an informal chat to a 'war and peace' detailed business plan, which has to all be documented on the firm's standard forms, followed up by numerous panel interviews.

Regardless of how your firm works, your Business Case will be strengthened if you include the following:

- Who am I going to target to win new business for the firm?

- How am I going to target them?

- How will I build my part of the business up so that it is sustainable and profitable? This includes how to win the clients and also how to build the team to service the work.

- What is the evidence that I can actually do all of this?

- How will I justify to my partners that the extra investment in me, and the fact that they will share profits with me, is going to be very worthwhile to them?

Typical format for a Business Case

Your firm may or may not have its own way that it wants you to present your Business Case. However, most firms are likely to require these details to be included in your Business Case:

Outline of your current practice

Your partners want to understand the value of your current practice. This means you will need to help them understand:

- The services you offer to your clients and the value you help them achieve.

- If you deliver a distressed service or transactional service like insolvency or litigation, then the value of your current Referral Networks. This means identifying your Top 10 referrers and breaking down the value of the work they send to you.

- The revenue you have billed for your Top 5–10 clients for each of the last 3 years.

- How your practice measures up against the metrics that your firm cares about? E.g. recoverability, billings.

- The current size of the team within your practice.

How you plan to grow your practice over the next 3 years

This is where you draw a picture of the opportunity that the partnership will have with your practice. In this you will need to show:

- The markets and geographies you plan to target and why you have chosen these; i.e. what is the opportunity available to the firm for targeting these markets and geographies?

- The services you will offer to your clients

- How you will compete and differentiate yourself from your key competitors

- How you will fuel the growth of your practice; for example, will this be by growing more of your current client portfolio? Winning new clients? Cross-selling your services to the firm's clients?

- What are the Goals that the partners could measure you on and which will demonstrate how you plan to grow your practice?

- Revenue and profit for your practice for the next three years, broken down by year

- Potential known risks which may stop you achieving your Business Case

- The team and people resources you will need to deliver the promise of your Business Case.

12-month marketing plan

This is your marketing plan to help you grow your practice to achieve the growth figures you are predicting for your practice. It will contain:

- Key account plans for the clients that you plan to grow materially in the next 12 months. These account plans will identify the opportunity with the client and your activity plan to realise this opportunity.

- Your prospective client list and your activity plan to convert these into clients.

- Your Networking Strategy to strengthen your Referral Networks.

- How you plan to build general awareness of you and what you do in the marketplace.

Critical success factors

This is where you identify:

- The support and budget you need to achieve your Business Case

- Any issues preventing or hindering the delivery of your Business Case; e.g. staffing, marketing budget, skill gaps.

Summary

This is a 3-sentence sell (see later in this chapter for how to write it), which succinctly articulates the commercial opportunity for the partnership with your Business Case.

 Use the Career Kitbag's examples of real business cases to help you start to create your own Business Case

Common mistakes people make with their Business Case

When our team works with clients on their Business Cases it is not uncommon to find these mistakes in their first drafts. In reality, some of these mistakes can't be fixed overnight.

Too focused on their technical ability

By the time you get to partner your technical ability is pretty much taken as a given. Being seen as a 'good lawyer' or a 'great technician' is all very well. Demonstrating that the firm will have a commercial advantage by making you up to partner normally doesn't involve an exploration of your technical skills. Your firm is more interested in how you will market your skill set in order to build up a business.

Not enough evidence

Far too often Business Cases are written along the lines of *I'm a good person, I've done some good work and my clients like me*. This is what most firms would expect of their most senior non-partner fee earners. It is not enough to justify why your partners should start to share the profits of the firm with you. Unfortunately not everyone has the evidence yet that they have a robust Business Case, because this takes time to build up.

Case Study: Jay

After Jay had spoken with some of the equity partners in his firm, he discovered that he didn't need to have a junior partner-sized client portfolio to get recommended for partner. He did need to have built several Referral Networks. But just having the Referral Networks was not enough on its own; he needed to have proof that these Referral Networks were strong enough to already be feeding him, and the rest of the firm, new profitable client business.

Not targeted enough

I once made a joke that far too many small firm accountants would go after any client with a pulse and a tax return. This was a joke, but there may have been an element of truth to this statement. It is not just accountants who struggle to accurately define their ideal target market and then focus their marketing on this segment. Lawyers and consultants are just as guilty. Far too often woolly words, such as 'small business owners', 'SMEs', 'entrepreneurs' or 'high net-worth individuals' are used to describe the type of clients that people want to attract. For example, an entrepreneur could be someone who sells a few of their homemade jams at a farmers market or Richard Branson. A Business Case with a tightly defined target client will demonstrate:

- This is the niche I am going to focus on

- These are the prospects I am going to actively work to convert to clients
- This is how my marketing activities will help me get in front of my prospects
- These are the timescales for when new clients and fees will be won.

Note: the next chapter will arm you with the tools to choose your niche and then target it effectively.

It doesn't address the 'Why me' and 'Why now' questions

Your Business Case needs to address why your partners should make *you* up to partner *this* time around. After all, if there is a good opportunity in the marketplace, there is nothing to say that your firm should choose you to go after that opportunity. Or go after this opportunity this time around. This is why it is vitally important that you show how you are the best-placed person to seize the opportunity now, which is what you will outline in your Business Case.

Case Study: Jem

Jem was a director of sales for a large US consultancy firm. He had a track record of helping the firm sign up clients worth hundreds of millions of dollars. He asked me to help him with his pitch for partnership as he wasn't a typical candidate for partnership in his firm. The question I put to him was, *Why should your firm make you up to partner?* After all, without having partner on his business card he was already winning massive pieces of client business. We spent a fair amount of time working out the reasons why the firm would benefit from having him in the partnership, and why they should make him partner now. As a result of this conversation, the chairman of his firm told him that his was the best pitch they had ever seen for partnership.

Too much superfluous detail

When you are aiming to prove your worthiness for partnership, it can be easy to try to communicate every single scrap of detail and evidence that proves your case. This is one of the most common mistakes that people make with their Business Case. Too much detail often has the opposite effect by diluting your key evidence. Your partners should not be made to work too hard to understand how you will give them a commercial advantage by being made up to partner.

How to build your Business Case if you are currently in industry

People in industry who are looking to make a career change and go for partner regularly contact me for advice on how to demonstrate a Business Case. They may have been in practice at some point in their career, but what they lack is the evidence that they can easily create a client following.

If you haven't had to sell to people outside of your organisation then you can't just magic up evidence that you will be able to attract and convert the right type of clients for the firm. What you can do is recall examples of when you have had to be persuasive and influence people, inside and outside of your organisation, to follow a course of action. If you have been, for example, the General Counsel or Finance Director then you will be persuading people in your organisation on a daily basis.

One of the benefits to firms of bringing in lateral hires at partner level from industry is their network of contacts through their industry. Therefore in the 12–24 months before you plan to make the move into practice focus on building up a very strong network of contacts. These contacts should be people who have the authority to buy or are highly influential in the buying process for your potential firm's services both inside and outside of your firm.

Note: in Chapter 9 we look at how you can build up strong Referral Networks.

How to build up a Business Case if you are non-fee earning

If you are in a role where you are not client facing, it can be tricky to put together a Business Case. After all, in this scenario you can't build a Business Case based on the client work you will win or service. In other words you need to think slightly more laterally about the advantage your partnership will gain if you are made up to partner. What will they gain or what potential pain will they avoid by making you up to partner?

Normally your Business Case needs to prove things along these lines:

The benefit to the practice of you being privy to partners' conversations, around the partnership table, significantly earlier than you are now

Typically this takes the form of showing that if you are involved in the conversations earlier it results in less work and heartache for the partners. Normally, these conversations are the big ones, which have a material impact on the firm's strategy, bank balance or structure, and often requiring a Partnership Vote.

If you can show some real examples of the impact – whether good or bad – of you being involved earlier, or brought in too late, in crucial partnership conversations, this will strengthen your Business Case considerably. For example, this could be an aborted firm merger, that if you had known about it earlier you could have advised them much quicker that this was not a good opportunity for the firm.

Why you and your team will provide a better service to the practice if you have a more influential position

Typically you and your team need to be viewed positively by the partners before you can even begin to think about making partner. This part of the Business Case is where you demonstrate how positively your team is viewed by the partners/firm as a whole. Then you offer up potential ideas of how *better* a service your team could provide if you were able to be more proactive and less reactive. You would only be able to be more proactive if you had more sight of the potential projects, mergers, business plans and strategy changes as they were being conceived rather than when they had been officially ratified.

Look at precedents set by your well-performing competitors

The reality is that before you can be made partner in your firm there normally needs to be a mindset shift from your partners. After all many partners are not comfortable with having partners who have no fee-earning responsibilities. What many partners fear is getting left behind by firms, which they see as peers. If you can show how your competitors have started to perform better than you by having non-fee earners within the partnership structure, this will considerably strengthen your Business Case.

A 6-step process to help you communicate your Business Case in an impactful but succinct way

It is not unusual to be given very short notice, i.e. less than two weeks to prepare a Business Case for partnership. For example, I'd been chatting via e-mail with a lawyer who was given one week's notice that she was being put up for partner. It meant she was slightly flustered as she was expected to write her entire Business Case in a week. In an ideal world your Business Case will be written over a series of months after consulting with the great and good of the partnership. However, life doesn't always work out like that!

This 6-step process will help you articulate your Business Case.

Step 1. What is your firm aiming to achieve?

It is surprisingly common for a firm to have a very vague and shrouded-in-mystery process to get onto and through Partner Track. Firms like the Big 4, BDO and Grant Thornton have a very clear and transparent process for Partner Track, but these firms are unfortunately in the minority. Many mid-tier and small 'traditional partnerships' will get sponsoring partners to write the Business Case for the person they are sponsoring. The first that the new partner hears about being on Partner Track, is when they are congratulated on making partner!

If you are going to write an effective Business Case you need to know what the stated or unstated headline strategy is for the firm. What is their long-term aim for growth or survival? The best Business Cases make a strong link between the firm's strategy and how their Business Case will help the firm achieve its strategy.

A firm will always have a long-term strategy. It could be as simple as 'do more of the same'. Sometimes it is never openly articulated. If you are going to be a member of the partnership you need to know what this strategy is – and there may be different versions of this strategy depending on who you speak to!

Step 2. Identify how you will help strengthen the partnership and increase the profits as a partner

This is where you identify the 'Why you', but in the context of what the partnership is trying to achieve. For example, what other needed skills or experiences will you bring to the partnership. For example, perhaps you could demonstrate how you would help your partnership strengthen its regional networks to get its desired greater geographic coverage.

Step 3. Build your 1-sentence sell and 3-sentence sell

In one sentence sum up why the partnership should make you partner. This will not be easy, but it will help you get crystal clear on the message you want to get through in your Business Case for partnership *and* pitch at the Partnership Panel Interview. It could possibly be something like this:

> *My relationship with the Tesco account will grow into a partnership-sized portfolio and help the firm fulfil its strategy of a strong retail sector team.*

Now expand this 1 sentence to 3 sentences, which is your short pitch for 'Why me' for partner.

> *My relationship with the Tesco account has grown the account for tax by 50% and £200,000 over the last 2 years. As a result of my internal network within Tesco, I have grown, on behalf of the firm, a pipeline of £500,000-750,000 of additional work. The work I lead within Tesco gives us good credentials to exploit opportunities in the retail marketplace worth over £5 million to the firm over the next 2 years.*

This discipline of making every word fight to be included will force you to think very clearly and succinctly about your Business Case and Personal Case.

Step 4. Storyboard your 3-sentence pitch

Before you are tempted to delve into the detail, it is time to storyboard your 3-sentence pitch. What you want to do is tell the story of your Business Case, without extra unnecessary detail.

One of the best ways to do this is take 5–10 slides, and use only the slide titles to tell the headline story of your Business Case for partnership. There will typically be the order of:

> 3-sentence pitch
>
> Reason 1 which supports/qualifies 3-sentence pitch
>
> Reason 2 which supports/qualifies 3-sentence pitch
>
> Reason 3 which supports/qualifies 3-sentence pitch
>
> Risk of not promoting you to partner this time

For example:

> Slide 1:
>
> *My relationship with the Tesco account has grown the account for tax by 50% and £200,000 over the last 2 years. As a result of my internal network within Tesco, I have grown, on behalf of the firm, a pipeline of £500,000-750,000 of additional work.*

The work I lead within Tesco gives us good credentials to exploit opportunities in the retail marketplace worth over £5 million to the firm over the next 2 years.

Slide 2:

My relationship with the Tesco account has grown the account for tax by 50% and £200,000 over the last 2 years

- Tesco account worth £400k in FY 12/13, now worth £600k in FY 14/15

- Growth driven by securing all of Tesco VAT and Transfer Pricing work

Slide 3:

As a result of my internal network within Tesco, I have grown, on behalf of the firm, a pipeline of £500,000-750,000 of additional work.

- Built strong relationships with Tesco Head of Tax, UK Supply Chain Director, Head of Tesco Personal Finance

- Relationships have allowed us to pitch for 3 corporate finance projects worth £500-750k for the firm. In 2 projects we are the only firm pitching.

Slide 4:

The work I lead within Tesco gives us good credentials to exploit opportunities in the retail marketplace worth over £5 million to the firm over the next 2 years.

- The work I do in Tesco can be replicated in the rest of the top 3 UK based supermarkets. Have already received one enquiry to help Waitrose with a similar work.

- The consolidation in the large electrical goods and DIY retailers means there are opportunities within this part of the retail sector.

Slide 5:

Why make me partner this time?

- The people I deal with client side expect to be working with a partner of the firm. If I am not a partner this time, it will negatively impact our chances of exploiting the current opportunities in the retail sector.

- Making me up to partner would give me the time to spend more time on business development to be able to grow my tax practice.

Step 5. Fill in the detail to support the titles on each slide

Your aim when filling in the detail for each slide is to still keep your words punchy and succinct. Don't fall into the trap of making the font smaller and smaller to fit all those words onto the slide. It should not be *War and Peace*! The whole point of forcing you to use this method is that it helps you cut out the waffle and make each word really count.

Step 6. Expand your storyboard into a full Business Case

Now take what you have written and expand it as much as is necessary to give the partners the detail that they require within your Business Case. See earlier in this chapter for what most firms want to see in a Business Case.

This process can be used to give you all the information you need to prepare your pitch for partnership in your Partnership Interview.

The commercial realities of inheriting a partner's portfolio

One of the easier ways of justifying your Business Case is to take over the portfolio of a retiring partner. However, the actual challenge of growing and sustaining the client portfolio is a lot harder in the long term. The stark truth of the matter is most advisors' clients are within 10 years of their age. Therefore, if a partner retires at 60, there is a good bet that their networks of referrers and clients have already retired or are thinking about winding down for retirement. When a client finds that they will be working with another advisor, then this can be a strong factor in them deciding to have a look in the marketplace to see if someone else can service their needs better. Brokers, who sell books of business for accountants, factor in that at least 20% of the clients will leave when the book of business is sold to a new accountant.

When a professional gets towards retirement there often isn't the incentive or motivation to carry on growing their portfolio. As a consequence some clients may have already drifted off and opportunities with the current client portfolio will have been missed. Therefore, even if you are handed a partner-sized client portfolio on a plate you need to still think very carefully about:

- How you will keep the profitable clients
- How you will grow the existing client portfolio
- How you will go out and find your own clients
- How to plan and gradually implement the handover between you and your retiring partner
- How to come out of the shadows of the partner you have taken over from.

Summary

Before the partnership can admit any new partner they need to have a Business Case for doing so. Your Business Case is where you demonstrate the commercial advantage of making you up to partner.

A robust Business Case is one where you clearly evidence how you will create a profitable client portfolio, which will give your firm a compelling competitive advantage. In your Business Case you need to visibly answer the questions of 'Why should I be made up to partner?' and 'Why should I be made up to partner this time around'

Action Points

1. Talk with the partners in your part of the practice. Find out their views on when the practice will need another new partner.

2. Identify the minimum size of your client portfolio you will need to gain the support of your Sponsoring Partner to be recommended for partnership.

3. Find out the process – particularly the forms – your firm uses to assess potential partners' Business Cases.

4. Book time with partners outside of your practice area to consult with them on your proposed Business Case for partner.

5. Start collating the evidence you will need for your Business Case.

6. Ask your Mentor and Sponsoring Partner what they did to prove their Business Case for partner.

7. If you have already started to create your Business Case, use the 6-step process in this chapter to create a 1-sentence and 3-sentence sell.

8. Use the 6-step process to create a short slide deck to pitch your Business Case.

9. Get someone to review your Business Case to identify how you can strengthen both your case and how you will present it.

Further resources

BOOKS

These books will help you build a strong Business Case for partner:

- *The Go-To Expert: How to Grow Your Reputation, Differentiate Yourself from the Competition and Win New Business*, Heather Townsend and Jon Baker, ISBN 978-1292014913

- *Influence: The Psychology of Persuasion*, Robert Cialdini, ISBN 978-0061241895

- *Rainmaking: Attract New Clients No Matter What Your Field*, Ford Harding, ISBN 978-1598695885

WEBSITES

- Advice and guidance on how to create and write a Business Case, including real business cases, plans and templates at: http://www.howtomakepartner.com

8

How to become the Go-To Expert

Topics covered in this chapter:

- The 3 Steps to becoming the Go-To Expert
- How to choose and commit to a niche
- Researching your niche
- How to package your brand so you become very appealing to clients in your niche
- How to use content to reinforce your expertise

" Don't blame the marketing department. The buck stops with the chief executive.

JOHN D ROCKEFELLER

If you are going to build up your own client portfolio you will need to build a strong enough personal brand to become a destination for work in your own right. Differentiating yourself from your peers and partners, internally and externally, is the challenge that every professional faces. What you can't do as a partner is rely on others to feed you work. Therefore, this means in your Business Case – even if you are inheriting a partner's client portfolio – you have to demonstrate how you personally will win new clients for the firm. As one Top 100 law firm managing partner said to me, anyone who wanted to become partner in *his* practice would need to demonstrate a sustainable track record of bringing in new clients to the firm. One way of solving this challenge is to become *the* advisor that clients want to work with, by growing a reputation as *the* Go-To Expert.

Being recognised as the Go-To Expert makes it easier to build up a strong business case. This is because being known as a Go-To Expert allows you to charge higher fees and spend less time on business development – after all, your reputation and profile in the marketplace and your firm is enough to generate enquiries on its own. If you do grow a strong brand in the marketplace as the Go-To Expert you will be amazed how quickly the partners in your firm will sit up and take notice of what you are doing. Pursuing a Go-To Expert strategy may be your ticket to make partner.

Note: this chapter is a summary of the essential elements of my previous book *The Go-To Expert*[6]

The 3 Steps to becoming the Go-To Expert

Whatever route you take to become the Go-To Expert, there will be 3 Steps. These are:

1. Choose and commit to your niche

2. Package up your brand so it becomes irresistible to your ideal client

3. Building your profile within your chosen marketplace and firm.

Step 1: How to choose and commit to your niche

What do we mean by a niche?

❝ By becoming an expert to a niche we become more important and valuable to our clients in the niche.

    ALAN STEVENS, AUTHOR OF PING, THE POCKET MEDIA COACH

---

6   *The Go-To Expert: How to Grow Your Reputation, Differentiate Yourself from the Competition and Win New Business*, Heather Townsend and Jon Baker, ISBN 978-1292014913

The dictionary defines *niche* as:

- A situation or activity specially suited to a person's interests, abilities or nature

- Relating to or aimed at a small specialised group or market.

When we talk about your niche in this book, we are referring to these definitions of a niche; i.e. where your particular passion and technical talents are used to cater for one particular specialist audience. Without a niche, clients will see you as identical to your peers. When you establish a niche of your own, it allows you to easily differentiate yourself and rapidly grow your profile and reputation in your chosen marketplace.

Your niche is just one part of your Personal Brand. However, your niche and how well you capitalise on your niche will heavily influence the rest of your Personal Brand; i.e.

- How you communicate to the external world

- How you choose to dress when in 'professional' mode

- The technology you choose to adopt; for example, are you an Apple or an Android person?

Why you need you to be committed to your niche

Reason 1: It helps you rather than your partner or peers be referred and recommended more often

The recent rapid growth and adoption of social media has led to people being able to quickly generate a strong profile in their network and the marketplace. Social media is also enabling people to maintain networks vastly bigger than a network based on face-to-face interactions alone. Five years ago you may have only had one or two people within your network that you would be happy to recommend. Today, you are only one click or Google search away from generating five or six recommendations of people within your network. It's the strength and marketability of your Personal Brand, which is the determining factor whether you, rather than other partners in your practice, will be the person that others recommend.

Case Study: Geoff

Geoff was looking to build up a specialism in sports law. He knew that his firm's sports law sector team was looking for a financial advisor who had credibility in advising golfers and ultra-high net-worth individuals from the world of sport. Geoff asked me whether I knew anyone. As it happens I had worked with a client who was a financial advisor who specialised in advising golfers. Even though I hadn't spoken with this client for a few years, he was instantly recallable and I made the introduction. Referrals have now started to flow between the financial advisor and the sports law team.

Reason 2: It helps your marketing materials be more effective

When you are clear about the target market for your niche, your marketing materials become more effective. This is because you know:

- Where to place your marketing materials and content so that your niche reads it
- The right buttons to press to build an emotional connection with your audience which compels them to take action quickly; e.g. contact you
- How to package up your services so that they are a strong fit to solve your niche's problems.

Reason 3: It can help you define new opportunities for business

Growth opportunities can come when you define your niche, since the niche leads your thinking and whole approach into areas you may never have fully considered before.

Reason 4: It enables you to differentiate yourself from your peers

Look at any accountant, lawyer or consultant's website and you will find it will probably mention most of these words:

- Proactive

- Speak your language

- Value for money

When you compare one technical specialist with a competitor, it's often very difficult to differentiate them from each other. This is why you need to be niched. In the *FT Effective Client Advisor Relationships Report*[7], they found that 40% of buyers of professional services have being a sector specialist in their Top 3 buying criteria, and 67% of buyers want to work with an advisor who has a deep understanding of their business and marketplace.

Reason 5: It allows you to tailor your service to what your clients want and need, making it easier to convert prospects to clients

When you adopt a niche you can tailor the services you offer very closely to your niche's needs, lifestyle and problems. This makes it easier for clients to choose to work with you rather than another fee earner in your firm or a competitor.

Reason 6: It helps you to form strategic alliances

One of the easiest ways for any professional to win work is to form strategic alliances with other professionals offering complementary services.

Reason 7: It minimises client churn

If your clients know and believe that you truly understand their needs and requirements – plus speak their language – they are less likely

---

7   *FT Effective Client–Adviser Relationships Report 2012* – http://ftcorporate.ft.com/professional-services-2/

to be attracted away to one of your generalist competitors with a cheaper alternative solution.

Case Study:
The Franchise Surgery

The Franchise Surgery is a series of surgeries for existing franchisors to come in and speak to professional advisors who specialise in franchising. The surgery was set up by Carl Reader, an accountant who specialises in franchising. For each surgery, they tend to get 6–10 franchisors. Every professional advisor in attendance normally comes away with invoiceable business from each surgery session.

How to choose your niche

Some professionals find that by the time they get to Partner Track they already have a clearly defined niche. However, this isn't the case for everyone.

Case Study:
Michael

Michael spent 10 years in the retail industry, initially within store management and then moved into HR. He enjoyed the employment law side of what he did so much he decided to re-train as a lawyer and join a top 50 UK law firm. As a result of his HR background he qualified into employment law and was poached by his firm's retail sector team. As a result of working almost exclusively with his firm's retail sector team he grew a deep expertise in employment law issues for retailers. He rapidly then progressed his career to partner as he became known as the Go-To Expert for employment law issues within retail companies.

If your work has been of a very generalised nature up to now, it can be hard to pin down what your niche will be. Remember your niche can be focused on a sector, specific location, technical specialism or even a type of person. There are only a few rules about choosing your niche:

1. You need to be able to build a Referral Network and highly targeted marketing plan based around the niche

2. There needs to be enough of a marketplace for you to build a partner-sized client portfolio

3. By claiming a niche it needs to significantly reduce the size of the marketplace you are focusing on.

Picking up on the last rule, far too many professionals say they have a niche or a specialism because they focus on 'owner-managed business', 'high net-worth individuals', 'SMEs' or 'Entrepreneurs'. These specialisms are not a niche as most of their peers will say that they also specialise in these. A true niche will typically dig one or two layers deeper than what everyone else says that they specialise in. As Nigel found, even though his marketplace was owner-managed businesses, he targeted his marketing on owner-managed businesses who:

1. Had 2–4 directors

2. Had 20–200 employees

3. Were manufacturing companies

When you are considering your niche you want to think about three factors:

- Passion

- Credibility

- Fit

All three factors need to be present for the niche to be right for you.

Case Study: Julia

Julia, an accountant, spent nearly a year agonising over the right niche for her. She loved socialising and spending time with coaches, trainers and consultants. She'd even worked with a few of these clients. However, because she wasn't passionate about the compliance-led type of work that these clients needed, she initially struggled to commit to this niche. It was only when Julia got to know these clients at a much deeper level that she realised they needed, and were prepared to pay, for her to work with them as a part-time Finance Director. From this point onwards, Julia committed to her niche and found it easy to win new clients within her niche.

Passion

Very simply, you need to be passionate about your niche if you are going to commit to it for the next few years at least. Clients want to work with someone who is enthusiastic and excited to be working with them and their personal or business affairs. If you don't have the heart for what you will doing you will never have the commitment or energy to build your profile and reputation within the niche.

Credibility

The easiest way to win new clients is when you already have a track record of working on similar types of clients. It is much easier to build up a client portfolio in a particular niche if you have an established network and verifiable results working with this type of client.

Fit

You may be passionate about a certain niche and have credibility within the niche, however, you need to feel as if you fit. This means that you have shared values, you care about what your clients truly care about and you find it easy to socialise with your clients.

Researching your niche

Before you can actively start to grow your profile you need to put yourself in your clients' shoes and understand what is going on in their world. When you do this, you can then be sure that you are offering the right services. Plus you can be confident that you are communicating through your marketing and general content the material things that your ideal client wants and needs.

It can be very tempting to skip this step and just assume you know what they want, need and are interested in.

Case Study: Phil

Phil, an accountant in a UK mid-tier firm, set out to become the Go-To Expert for Independent Retail Businesses. He got a rich source of priceless insight when he took the time to talk with clients and prospects to get their view of the world. This insight enabled him to create highly tailored content and packaged accounting and advisory services. 12 months after doing this research, a significant proportion of his new clients came to him because of the independent retailer focused content he created and shared.

There are many different ways you can get to know your target client:

- Reading the trade-related press, blogs, on-line forums and articles

- Following companies and individuals from your niche market on social media; e.g. LinkedIn, Twitter, Facebook, Google+

- Attending relevant industry events, such as conferences and seminars

- Interviewing people who work within the industry, particularly your existing clients
- Running focus groups for people within the industry or customers/clients of your niche market
- Sending out a survey or questionnaire. You will get a better response rate if you share anonymised results of the survey with all participants.
- Reading on-line forums
- Reading the websites, blogs, reports and white papers provided by your competitors
- Signing up for newsletters/blogs from your competitors and people in your niche market

What you want to find out in your research

You want to understand what your prospective clients are thinking and are interested in, as they go through their journey as a buyer. The journey a person makes before they buy from an external supplier tends to have 5 discrete stages:

1. Everything is fine

This is the stage when your buyer has no need of your services. It could be that everything is absolutely fine without the proverbial cloud in the sky. Or that if they do have problems they need to fix they are already working on them with an internal resource or an external supplier.

2. I know I have some problems

Your buyer has now moved on to knowing that he or she has a problem. Now this could be a minor niggle which they are happy to ignore, or a full-blown crisis, which they need to fix right now. Part of your research will establish what problems they are motivated to solve, and which ones they are motivated to solve by using an external supplier. When you know the problems they are coming up against, you can bet that they will be consciously or sub-consciously looking for answers to their problems. If your content will help them find the answers or demonstrate to them that they have a problem that needs to be fixed, you will have started the process of generating a lead. A lead is normally defined as a Prospective Client who has identified himself or herself to you as being interested in using your services.

The types of problems that clients will be driven to buy your services for are Pain Points. The reasons why they decide to do something about these Pain Points will often be rooted in a deep-seated emotional rather than rational reason. For example, a business owner is unlikely to buy more advisory services from an accountant because they want to grow their business. The real reason they want to grow their business will be more emotional, such as "I want to build a business with a capital value of £1 million to provide me with a pension fund", and therefore they need an accountant.

3. I have decided what I need to do about my problem.

Now that your buyer has found answers to his or her problem he or she will have a clear idea of the outcome they want. This could be as simple as do nothing, or call in the consultants to help them on a multi-million pound 3-year project. At this stage they may not have decided exactly how they will solve their problem. What they have decided is the desired outcome they require. A typical buyer at this stage will have very rational questions they want to answer, such as:

- Who can help me fix my problem?
- How much will it cost?
- What are the risks with choosing each particular course of action?
- What are the steps in the process to fix my problem?

4. Finding people to help me and choosing the right solution

It is at this point that most buyers will actively look for a supplier to help them decide on the right solution to solve their problem. They will then spend time with a selection of suppliers to refine their ideal solution and decide who is the right person to help them achieve it. If the buyer has been engaging with you (or your content) much earlier in their journey, it is very likely that they will actively make contact with you to see how you can help them.

Part of your research will help you identify the services you need to offer to attract clients. A way to stand out from your competitors is to name your services in language that your ideal clients will instantly see how it helps them.

Case Study: Jenner

Jenner is a litigator. His niche is in helping fund managers, and he found during his research that his Investment Banking clients were constantly receiving potential malpractice claims. 95% of these claims were normally spurious, but still needed some action. As a result he offered a retainer service to his clients so they could call him and quickly see which claims could be easily sent packing, and which ones had some merit and would need to be carefully handled.

5. Taking the decision to buy

The buyer has now decided on a solution and the supplier they will use to help them achieve their desired outcome. Very often this point in the buying journey is known as the 'closing the deal' part of the process. Your research in this stage ideally will find out how to make it easier to close the deal. Will you need to offer a guarantee? Maybe you need to think about your payment terms? Will some element of a conditional fee agreement help more clients sign up?

Doing research interviews on your niche

One of the most valuable ways to complete your research, and probably the most daunting way, is to do a series of research interviews. Here are some tried and tested tips to get agreement to do these interviews:

- Don't make it about you and what you need. Your reason for doing them is to understand the niche and their business in more depth so you and your firm can better tailor your services to that niche.

- Don't ask for too much. Most people will say *yes* to a 15-minute or even 30-minute phone call. Go with the availability in their diary, not when you have time to talk.

- Send the questions in advance and keep them short and open-ended.

- Don't give any hint of wanting to sell to them. Make this absolutely clear from the outset.

- Offer to send a summary of your findings to them.

Here are some good questions that have been used very successfully in niche research interviews with prospective clients and current clients:

- What are the top 3 challenges you are working on right now in your business? How are they impacting what you do at an individual, functional and organisational level?

- What are the top 3 barriers to growth that you are facing right now?

- Given the benefit of hindsight, what do you wish someone had told you 1–2 years ago?

- What 3 ways is technology changing your business but also your clients and customers' expectations?

- What are the 3 biggest shifts in your marketplace, which may change the way you do business?

- At what point, or what would need to happen, for you to use the services of someone similar to me?

- What 3 things do you see as the biggest threat to you and your business's future success?

- If you were in my shoes, who else would you recommend I ask these questions to?

Research interviews are not something that you do once. They become more powerful if you do one or two of them each month. The insight they bring you will help you polish and hone your marketing, in particular the content they want to read, watch and listen to. From personal experience, it is not unusual to flush out some new client leads as a result of doing the interview.

Using the results of your niche research

The results of your client research will now help you:

- Decide on the opportunities in the niche for your services
- Identify the services you need to offer to capitalise on these services
- Build a content plan and strong on-line footprint to help you increase your credibility with Prospective Clients.

Step 2: How to package your brand so you become very appealing to clients in your niche

Now that you have completed your research and chosen your niche, it is time to package your brand. This means you need to build a strong on-line footprint, with highly targeted content and decide on which tailored services to offer to your Prospective Clients.

How to create a strong on-line footprint

Your Prospective Clients are most likely to check you out on your firm's website, LinkedIn and other social media sites, and to be googling your name. This means that anything you create in the on-line world needs to help your Prospective Clients answer these questions *about you*:

- Do you understand their world?

- Are you credible and what evidence do you present to prove it?

- What results could you help them achieve?

- Are you trustworthy?

- Can they understand more about you as a person and see themselves wanting to build a relationship?

 Use the Career Kitbag's 'Guide to crafting a LinkedIn profile', which will help you use LinkedIn to win new clients

Note: later on in this chapter we look at how to use valuable content to reinforce your expertise.

How to decide on what tailored services to offer your clients

The easy answer is to offer services that your niche clients really want to buy. The research you have already completed should give you a clear indication of what clients are prepared to buy and potentially how much they are willing to spend on these services. Here are some more guidelines to help you decide on what services to offer:

Have a range of services at different price points

It is very rare for a client to buy a high-priced service from you immediately. It is almost always the situation where they will try you out first, maybe by having a preliminary conversation with you or buying a small almost 'risk-free' service. What services, potentially complementary, can you offer to your prospective clients to encourage them to take the first step to buy from you? These are often badged as an 'audit', 'review' or 'diagnostic'.

Case Study: Peter

Peter is an IP lawyer specialising in life sciences companies. He identified that the government was offering grants to companies to help them pay for an IP audit. He now tends to sell the audit first which – as it is mostly funded by the government grant – tends to have a very high uptake. The results of this audit then give him the knowledge to help his clients prioritise and plan what work needs to be done in a timescale and budget to suit them.

Make your services 'stand out'

Far too many professionals use their own language, rather than their client's language, to describe their services. If you really want to stand out, name your services in your client's language. For example:

Company Commercial Legal Services becomes *'buying and selling your business'*

Management Accounts becomes *'putting you back in control of your numbers'*

Credit Control becomes *'getting you paid fully on time'*

Tailor the features of your service

It is often the features of your service that will truly set yourself apart from your competitors. How can you enhance or tailor your services so that it becomes highly attractive to your Prospective Clients?

Case Study:
Sarah

Sarah helps ultra-high net-worth clients buy and sell residential properties. As well as doing all the standard conveyancing service she offers a comprehensive range of complementary services. For example she:

- Will help them access the finance needed to buy the property

- Advise on how to buy or sell their property in a tax efficient way

- Does accompanied visits to potential properties with their client or their representative.

Case Study:
Joseph Frasier Solicitors

Joseph Frasier specialise in working with deaf and hard-of-hearing clients. Such people find it very difficult to work with solicitors as most solicitors require a face-to-face conversation or phone-based communication. So, Joseph Frasier have tailored their services to this niche by:

- Training all their staff in sign language

- Providing the option for their clients to talk to their solicitors by Skype message rather than having to use the phone

- Specialising in industrial deafness personal injury claims.

How to use Valuable Content to reinforce your expertise

To help clients find you at the early stages of their buying journey you will need to continually find and write Valuable Content, then share it with your target audience.

❝ If you continually share information that people actually value, clients and customers will choose to come to you.

SONJA JEFFERSON AND SHARON TANTON, AUTHORS OF
VALUABLE CONTENT MARKETING

What is meant by Valuable Content?

❝ Valuable Content is the focus of all good marketing today.

CHARLES H. GREEN

Content is any information you have written, videoed, recorded or shared such as:

- White paper
- Your own blog post or cross post to another blog
- Article in the press
- Quote in an article
- YouTube video
- Podcast
- Comment in a LinkedIn discussion
- Tweet or Facebook post
- Webinar
- Interview on radio or TV

- A book
- Seminar, event or festival presentations you have recorded
- Page on your website.

Anyone can write and share content, whereas, Valuable Content is anything that you share which your target audience will find valuable. For example, if you are an IP lawyer for coaches and trainers, a valuable piece of content for them would be bespoke tips to help them protect their IP. Part of your Business Development Plan, within your Partner Track Plan, will be defining what content you will produce in what format.

The Internet has permanently changed how people buy professional services. Only ten years ago, all you had to do to become the Go-To Expert was get your name in the right place – write a book, regularly speak at events, have a 3-page brochure and use a sales team to follow up any telephone, e-mail or postal enquiries. Today's modern world moves at such a pace that clients want answers now – not three days later, not at next month's event. This is why people turn to the Internet first to get answers to questions, problems, challenges and opportunities.

❚❚ Content marketing – producing a steady stream of helpful content to your audience, distributed through social media – is the quickest way for a professional to establish their reputation.

LEE FREDERIKSEN, CO–AUTHOR,
PROFESSIONAL SERVICES MARKETING

To build up your Business Case you will need to create a library of Valuable Content that helps you get found and emphasises your credibility for what you do.

The 3 ways to create your Valuable Content

Given the many demands on your time whilst you are on Partner Track the biggest barrier you face in order to sustainably produce

Valuable Content is time. However with smart planning it is possible to efficiently produce content.

Generate:

This is original content that you have created from scratch. This could include:

- Blog posts; i.e. short articles between 500-1000 words
- Updates on LinkedIn, Twitter and Facebook where you post where you are, what you are thinking, what you are about to do, or pose a question to your followers
- White papers, reports, guides, workbooks, etc.
- Video interviews with your fee earners
- Conversations on Twitter and Internet forums
- Standard forms, questionnaires, methodologies for the work you do with clients.

Recycle:

This is repurposed or repacked content, which you have adapted from its original form. This could include:

- Recycling a piece of work you do for a client to use with others
- Publishing (with permission) another person's blog post onto your blog (which they have already published elsewhere) or vice versa
- Repackaging a white paper or report into several blog posts
- Repackaging a piece of existing content so that it is aimed at a target niche
- Creating a standard questionnaire to use with other clients based on a piece of client work you have just done
- Adapting a plan from a contact in a totally different industry to suit your own purposes.

As a guide, if you record an interview, it will take you an hour to plan and record. You should aim to create a podcast from the interview. Then use the audio transcription from the podcast to create several standalone blogs which each take you under 20 minutes to write and edit.

Curate:

This is where you filter or select/share other people's or your firm's content, which you think that your network, contacts, clients or social media followers will find valuable. This could include:

- Tweeting a link to a blog post or article (whether or not it is your own article)
- Retweeting someone else's content
- Sharing a link to a blog or article on LinkedIn
- Including copies of presentations, video clips, white papers, reports and guides on fee earner's LinkedIn profiles
- Sending out a valuable article to the highest value people in your network
- Creating a discussion on a LinkedIn group based on the key points contained in an article
- Using a newsletter to share interesting articles on a theme.

What is a Content Plan?

A Content Plan is a summary of the Topics, Audience, Timing and Formats for the Valuable Content you will produce over, say, the coming year.

Why is it useful?

A Content Plan helps you to think about and schedule your content in advance. This has many benefits including:

- Allowing you to align your content production with your Partner Track marketing plan

- Saving time as you are not thinking about what you need to write all the time

- Enabling you to ask other people to write the content you need, for the time you need it.

Questions to ask before writing a Content Plan

Before jumping into writing a Content Plan, it is always worth taking a step back, to think about some important questions that will help you save time in the long run.

- What is a realistic expectation for your on-going content creation?

- Where are your clients looking for information?

- What sort of questions or problems are your clients looking for answers to? (see the section on Research earlier in this chapter)

- What content can be created by you, other people in the firm and by outside (independent) sources?

- What infrastructure (e.g. blog, e-mail marketing software, etc.) do you have available to help deliver the content?

How do you build a Content Plan?

Typically your Content Plan will contain:

- Guides, reports, blog posts and white papers which help to demonstrate your credibility

- Briefing documents for Prospective Clients to help reduce the perceived barriers and risks to hiring you

- Published and self-published books and e-books

- Incentives for people to sign up to the mailing list on your firm's website

- Podcasts, videos, YouTube clips, recorded teleseminars and webinars

- Case studies, testimonials
- Things that can be sold to clients, or bundled up, to increase the perceived value of your service or product
- LinkedIn, Twitter or Facebook status updates
- Answers on Internet forums
- Contributions to discussion threads on Internet forums
- Comments on other people's blog posts
- Newsletters
- Weekly tips sent out by e-mail.

At first, creating content can be a very daunting task. Either you don't know what to create or you have so much to create it becomes overwhelming. As the saying goes, *Rome wasn't built in a day*, and it is the same with your Content Plan. Prioritise the creation of content which will help you achieve your business development goals quicker. For example, if you want to win more business from your existing clients, what content would help them realise that they need to take action with a problem they have? If your main priority with your business development is to make it easier and quicker to convert Prospective Clients, what content would help them take decisions quicker?

 Use the Career Kitbag's 'Guide to content planning' to help you regularly create your own content

Step 3: Building your profile within your chosen marketplace and firm.

There are many different routes to build your profile, for example:

- Networking
- PR
- Writing a book

- Speaking
- Running webinars and seminars

The next chapter explores how to build your profile within your network in order to build your client portfolio.

Note: It is outside the scope of this book to explore how to use each of these routes. In the resources section of the book, you will find further reading to help you use each route to build your profile.

Summary

To directly attract your own client opportunities you will need to tightly define your niche and have a deep understanding of what it takes for them to buy your services. This will significantly increase the effectiveness of your business development activities.

Creating and sharing content which your ideal clients find valuable, will help reinforce your expertise and generate new client leads. Your client research will help you identify the type of content that your ideal client will find highly valuable as they progress through their buying journey.

Action Points

1. Talk to established partners to find out how they found their niche and specialisms.

2. Ask the partners in your firm what industries, sectors or specialist skills are likely to be in demand by clients and the marketplace generally over the next 5 years.

3. Reflect on what work you really enjoy and for what type of clients – this is likely to become your niche and ideal client.

4. If you are resisting committing to a niche or specialism, spend time with your Mentor to identify the cause of your resistance.

5. Build a plan of how you will really get to know your ideal client. In your plan identify at least 3 people or organisations you would like to have as clients. Find out who in your network can introduce you to them and then do your research interviews.

6. Complete at least 3 research interviews to identify what your ideal clients are thinking, feeling or interested in as they progress through their buying journey.

7. Read the trade newspapers and magazines to increase your industry knowledge of one or two sectors for which you would like to become the Go-To Expert.

8. Within your Partner Track Plan, build your own Content Plan and in the plan identify 3 months worth of content that you would like to create or share. In your plan decide where and how you will share the content.

Further resources

BOOKS

These books will help you define and communicate your personal brand:

- *Juggling the Big 3 for Lawyers: A Career-building Plan to Develop Your Personal Brand, Client Business, and Leadership Mindset*, Jennifer Overhaus, ISBN 978-0956274502

- *Personal Branding for Brits: How to sell yourself to find a job and get on at work ... without sounding like an idiot*, Jennifer Holloway, ISBN 978-0957542808

- *Me 2.0: 4 steps to building your future*, Dan Schawbel, ISBN 978-1607147121

These books will help you become The Go-To Expert:

- *The Go-To Expert: How to Grow Your Reputation, Differentiate Yourself from the Competition and Win New Business*, Heather Townsend and Jon Baker, ISBN 978-1292014913
- *How to Build Your Reputation: The Secrets of Becoming the Go To Professional in a Crowded Market Place*, Rob Brown, ISBN 978-1905823116
- *Valuable Content Marketing: How to Make Quality Content the Key to Your Business Success*, Sonja Jefferson and Sharon Tanton, ISBN 978-0749465803

WEBSITES

For help with deciding what content to create and share, look at:

- http://www.valuablecontent.co.uk

If you want to dig deeper into your personal brand, look at

- Dan Schawbel's personal branding blog http://www.personalbrandingblog.com/
- Jennifer Holloway's website on personal branding http://www.jennifer-holloway.co.uk

9

How to build strong Referral Networks

Topics covered in this chapter:

- What is a Referral Network?
- Why build multiple strong Referral Networks
- How to build your personal Networking Strategy
- How to generate referrals via your network
- How to implement your Networking Strategy

*** We are living in a knowledge economy in which the first thing to recognise is no single person is smart enough by themselves to be genuinely successful.*

HAMISH TAYLOR, SHINERGISE PARTNERS LTD

In many partners' minds having strong Referral Networks is the best route to regularly winning new clients. I wouldn't disagree with this assumption! Referral Networks are groups of people who regularly send you new business. Consequently, having these Referral Networks is one of the ways to strengthen your Business Case for partnership. However, networking can be the biggest drain on your time. After all, very often firms expect you to network in your own time. This chapter will help you save time with your networking by helping you build a personal Networking Strategy using a 5-step process. Within the chapter we introduce you to a way of systematically generating referrals using the SERVICE framework.

Why build your network and community?

The reason that most professionals in practice are taught to network effectively at the start of their career is that it is *the* most effective way to build awareness, get found and generate opportunities. Sit in a cafe near your work and tune in to the chatter around you – chances are you'll overhear a conversation that goes something like this:

> *You are thinking of re-doing your website/contacting a recruitment consultant/changing accountants? The person you should be talking to is X, they are the Go-To Expert for this.*

Ask anyone who is considered to be a rainmaker in their firm and they will mention the value of their network in helping them build their reputation, extend their reach and get them recommended. Get your networking right and others will do the job of selling for you, spreading the word about your services, products or skills – your own sales force happy to spot opportunities on your behalf, and for free!

You could be the best professional out there, but if no one knows about you, how are you going to be found? That's why it is so important for any aspiring partner to develop and maintain a strong network of people who can help tell others about your services and skills.

Networking has always been a highly effective tool. As long as commerce has existed, traders have banded together for the common protection against enemies, to govern the conduct of trade, and help each other out. But in today's global, knowledge-based economy it has really come to the fore. We have far greater choice and access to people than ever before, but less time to spend on finding the right people. This is why people are now using their networks more and more, to help them rapidly get to the best solution at the first time of asking. With the rise of on-line networking via social media you can now build a far larger and more engaged network more easily and more quickly than ever before.

Building your own personal Networking Strategy

What is a Networking Strategy?

Effective business networking is the process of finding, building and maintaining mutually beneficial relationships. Your Networking Strategy details how you will achieve your Goals via your networking activities.

A clear and concise Networking Strategy will allow you to make the decisions as to *what* networking activities you will do; i.e. it is your *plan* for connecting to important people. There are 5 steps involved in creating your Networking Strategy.

1. Aim
2. Audit
3. Find
4. Build
5. Maintain

1. Aim:	2. Audit:	3. Find:	4. Build:	5. Maintain:
Decide what you want to achieve with your network and networking activities	Assess the suitability of your current networking activities to help you achieve your Aim	Identify people to add in to your network	Progress and deepen the right relationships	Keep your relationships strong and working for you.

Diagram 9.1: The 5 steps to building your own personal Networking Strategy

If you complete each stage, your networking strategy will almost write itself.

Step 1: Aim

In this instance your Aim is to use your network and networking activities to help achieve the Goals from your Partner Track Plan. If you don't have this Aim clear in your mind, it's going to make it very difficult to make your networking activities actually happen. You won't have sufficient motivation to do any or some of these things:

- Make the effort to go into LinkedIn regularly and join in the conversation
- Go into Twitter daily
- Head out to a networking event after a long, hard day in the office
- Pick up the phone and speak to someone you haven't connected to for a while.

Step 2: Audit

Now that you have the Aim of your network and networking activities identified, it is time to run an audit, where you review who is already in your network.

Many people think that they have to build a network from scratch. Actually, each of us naturally has our own network – and for many of us, there will be some great contacts within our current network who will be able to help us achieve our Goals, Milestones and Objectives. For example, Robert was a long-term member of his golf club. It was only after sitting down with a member of the club, David, that he realised David was a senior decision maker in a company that he wanted as a client.

Just because you have a network and are networking all the time, doesn't mean to say that you are doing it in an effective manner; i.e. spending time with the right people in the right places. This is why the second stage of building a Networking Strategy is to do a networking Audit. After all, you don't want to change anything that is working.

The best way to do a networking Audit is to draw out your Network Map. Begin by literally mapping out your ideal network. It's an exercise that will really help to focus you on *who* you want to meet, and how these people are going to help you make partner. Remember that your internal firm network is just as important a Referral Network as your external Referral Networks.

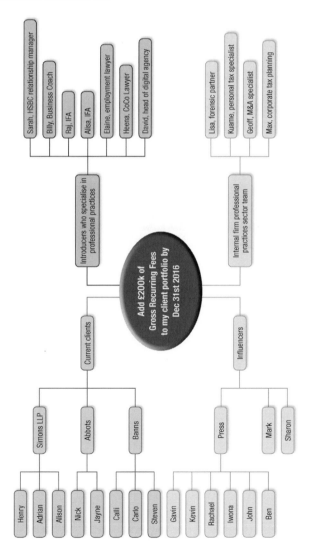

Diagram 9.2: Example of a Network Map

Use the Career Kitbag's 'Guide to Networking mapping' to help you create your own Network Map

This may sound rather calculating or manipulative. However, it is a tool to help you focus on how you will spend your networking time. Let's be frank here: how many times have you turned up to a networking event without knowing why you were there? Was it a productive use of your time? *No?* Did you ever consider finding out in advance who was attending, to identify key people to target? A Network Map will help you visualise your networking activities. It has the additional benefit of helping you prioritise your activities, because you now truly understand why you are networking and why it is important for your Business Case and Personal Case for partner.

Very often many professionals, after completing their Network Map, realise that their *current* network contains many of the types of people that can actively help them achieve their Goals, Milestones and Objectives.

Case Study: Steph

Steph was so determined to make partner that she did a regular audit of the people in her Referral Networks. If she had added 1 strategically important person to her list, she would automatically bump 1 or 2 people off the bottom. She wasn't quite that harsh, but she halved the frequency of seeing those people so that they took up less of her valuable time. It didn't take very long for her to be mixing mostly with excellent people, and this was strong point in her Business Case.

Once you have completed your Network Map it is now time to critically look at the effectiveness of your current networking activities. For example:

- What activities are you doing – such as membership of a professional networking group – which are helping you connect with the right types of people; i.e. hubs?

- What activities are you doing which are helping you build your Business and Personal Case

- What activities are not working for you?

- What activities should you start doing right now? That is, this week.

Step 3: Find

I often tell a story when delivering a keynote or masterclass on effective business networking about George Clooney. The story goes as follows:

People are always asking me who I want to meet – I guess this is an occupational hazard of writing a book on networking! I always answer, George Clooney. People then wonder why I answer George Clooney? The fact is, my ultimate aim is to become a kept woman. George Clooney represents someone who could shortcut my way to achieving that aim.

Now, everyone has someone who can help shortcut their way to achieving their Goals. For example, David Kaye, a retail legal specialist has found that his relationship with Philip Green, the founder of the Arcadia Group, has led to many referrals to clients in the retail sector.

Step 4: Build

Sadly, many professionals' viewpoint of networking is that it is all about the process of *finding* contacts.

> ❛❛ *Don't count your conversations. Make your conversations count!*
>
> ROB BROWN[8]

If you pulled open your desk drawer, how many business cards would prompt the thought *I was meant to get back to them?*

That's probably the biggest mistake professionals make with their networking activities. They focus too much on *finding* contacts rather

---

8   Author of How to Build Your Reputation – the secrets of becoming the 'go to' professional in a crowded marketplace

than deepening and maintaining the relationships, which will help them achieve their Goals, Milestones and Objectives via their network.

Once you have identified *who* you need to meet, then you need to categorise them. A simple A-, B- and C-list system works well where:

> *A-lister*: Someone who is likely to be able to help you achieve your networking goals in the short and medium term
>
> *B-lister*: Someone who is able to help you achieve your networking goals in the medium and long term
>
> *C-lister*: Someone who is unlikely to be able to help you achieve your networking goals

In your Networking Strategy, you need to decide on what you will do as a result of meeting an A-, B- or C-lister. Ideally you connect with everyone on LinkedIn and Twitter, even C-listers, as your or their circumstances may change.

For A-listers you:

- Start a Relationship Plan (see later on this chapter) for them, and diarise next steps from that plan
- Aim to speak in person to them at least once every 3 months
- Actively find ways to help them; for example, sending them articles which they will find useful
- Make at least one introduction and/or referral for them every 3 months
- Include them on a list on Twitter which you check every day.

For B-listers you:

- Find something useful to send to them at least every 3 months
- Aim to speak to them in person at least once a year.

The Excedia 5-level Relationship Model

The aim with your networking activity is to deepen those relationships that matter to you. Most people realise that not everyone is created equal in their Referral Network. In fact, the state of your relationship can be described in a 5-level Relationship Model, which allows you to categorise the state of your relationship:

Diagram 9.3: The Excedia 5-Level Relationship Model

Level 1: Identify

At this level, you have just become aware of this contact. Maybe someone has mentioned them in conversation or perhaps you have seen a tweet of theirs. Or perhaps they are on an attendance list of an event you are attending.

Level 2: Connect

At this point you have physically or virtually met a contact, and started a one- or two-way conversation; i.e. you have connected. For example, you may have talked to them at a face-to-face networking event, or exchanged some tweets or posts within an on-line forum.

Level 3: Engage

At this point, you have taken a conscious decision to strengthen the relationship, and move beyond small talk. This means that you have taken the time to have a one-to-one meeting with them, in person or by phone.

Level 4: Collaborate

The trust has built within the relationship to the point where you have agreed to help each other, pass referrals, and potentially actively look for ways to work together.

Level 5: Inner Circle

The relationship is now such that you have worked together, and regularly recommend each other's services. There is a strong possibility that your relationship has moved from a purely professional relationship into a personal friendship.

Relationship Plans

You want to have in place a Relationship Plan for all your A-listers and potentially some of your B-listers.

A Relationship Plan:

- Details what you know about the person and what more you want to know about them.

- Contains the desired level of contact you want.

- Indicates what you would like to achieve because of your relationship.

NAME	John Brown	LINKEDIN & TWITTER	www.linkedin.com/in/johnbrown @johnbrown
PHONE	01298 567 8910	WEBSITE	www.johnbrownllp.co.uk
EMAIL	jobrown@johnbrownllp.co.uk	ADDRESS	Business House, 100 Any Street, New Town AB10 9CD
ROLE	Owner	COMPANY	John Brown LLP
FREQUENCY OF CONTACT		In person: every 5 months, phone call: quarterly, email: monthly, twitter account monitored daily	
CURRENT & DESIRED RELATIONSHIP LEVEL (out of 5)		Current - 3, desired - 4	
THEIR GOALS & OBJECTIVES		1. In the next years double the size of their revenue and maintain profit margins 2. Identify 2 assistant solicitors to delegate work down too	
THEIR INTERESTS OUTSIDE OF WORK		Golf, fine dining, Spurs supporter	
FAMILY SITUATION		Married with 2 teenage children, Stephen (13), Alex (15)	
HOW CAN I HELP THEM?		Reduce tax bill and start to provide management accounts quarterly	
WHAT CONTENT DO THEY WELCOME ME SENDING THEM?		Our monthly newsletter & articles which they may find interesting	
RELATIONSHIP NEXT STEPS		Organise next lunch & suggest a round of golf	

Diagram 9.4: Example of a Relationship Plan

 Use the Career Kitbag's blank Relationship Plan to help you actively and effectively manage your own relationships

It's all very well having Relationship Plans for the folks who matter to you. However, you need to implement these plans. Every month review all of your Relationship Plans and check that you have 3 months of the right level of contact planned into your diary. Then, extend your Relationship Plans by another month.

Step 5: Maintain

Think back to your friends at school. How many of them are you still in contact with? Now of those that you have lost contact with, do you feel able to pick up the phone and speak with them? I'm guessing not. So, what has made the difference with your friends from school who you feel able to still pick up the phone and talk to?

Yes, regular communication. Without regular communication, your relationships will slip back and lose their usefulness. Therefore, a key part of your Networking Strategy needs to be *how* you will keep in touch with your network.

One of the best ways of keeping in touch with the important people in your network is through sending them and sharing with them Valuable

Content. This could be articles or recordings made by you or others. (See Chapter 8 for ideas on what content to send to them.)

How to generate referrals via your Referral Network

Having a strong Referrals Network is one thing, but using it to build a predictable marketing machine is quite another. Your personal Networking Strategy will get you talking to and in front of the right people, but if you don't say the right things, then you will miss out on opportunities to generate referrals via your network.

The SERVICE framework will help you use your networking activities to maximise the number of referrals you get through your network. SERVICE stands for:

Specific

Extraordinary Client Service

Relationships

Visibility

Initiative

Collaborate

Educate

Diagram 9.5: The SERVICE Referral Framework

Specific

In Chapter 8 it was recommended that you market to a specific niche. However to really reap the benefits of having a niche, you will need to commit to it. Therefore, when you are networking, remember to talk about your niche rather than claiming to be all things to all people.

Being specific is more than just being committed to your niche. It is also about being specific with your requests about who you want to be introduced to.

Extraordinary client service

One of the benefits of having a strong profile and Personal Brand or being seen as the Go-To Expert is the sheer volume of word-of-mouth recommendations you will generate. Indeed, Simone, a project director for the manufacturing sector, finds that every new client comes to her pretty much pre-sold on the basis of multiple personal recommendations. However, you will only get this word-of-mouth business if you deliver to clients not just good service, but extraordinary client service; the type of client service which just compels your clients to tell others about it. (Warning: if you don't deliver on the basics of client service then any attempt to deliver extraordinary client service will be wasted effort.) Luckily, extraordinary client service can be easily delivered fairly cheaply with just a little thought about what will make the difference to your clients. For example, how about:

- Keeping a stock of mobile phone rechargers in your office for when clients visit, so that they can charge their phone while they meet with you or your team.

- Taking note of your client's dietary preferences, so that you can always offer them a hot beverage and something to eat which they can drink/eat and will enjoy.

- Having some umbrellas in the office so you can walk clients out to their cars when it is raining.

- Sending them birthday cards.

- Introducing them to one potential client or referrer every six months.

- Sending them a small gift, relevant to the work you are doing, after your work is completed; e.g. a Conveyancing Solicitor sending a small food hamper to their clients on completion day.

Relationships

As already covered, a small core of relationships – your A-listers – will result in a large proportion of your referrals.

Visibility

Being seen in all the right places, whether on-line or off-line is a major component for referral generation. Your personal Networking Strategy will make sure that you are networking and being seen in all the right places.

Initiative

One of the best ways of generating referrals is to proactively ask for them, as well as introductions, which may lead to business. However, many of us don't feel we can ask, perhaps because it looks like we are being too pushy. Remember you are not directly asking for more business from them, just for their help:

> *I wonder whether you could help me? I'm looking for <insert the type of people you want to meet> who would also benefit from <insert the value you bring>.*

Here are good opportunities to ask for a referral:

- When a client gives you good feedback
- At the end of an assignment which has gone well
- When the client has recognised that you have gone over and above the call of duty for them.

When clients or people in your network give you referrals or introductions, ask their permission to use their name when making contact. Or even, suggest that you could prepare an introduction for them to use via the phone or e-mail.

Collaborate

Working together with other professionals who share the same niche market as you can be one of the most powerful ways to generate referrals. Who do you know who has a similar type of client base to you, but offers a different service? In the early days of your relationship you may want to help each other out with little things such as:

- Writing blog posts for each other
- Quoting them in an article
- Mentioning or recommending them in your newsletters.

As the relationship, trust and credibility build, it's worth thinking about bigger things you can do together, such as:

- Launching a joint service or product
- Running a marketing event or campaign together
- Systematically introducing all your new clients to them, with an easy incentive to use their services.

Educate

If you want your Referral Network to act as an unpaid sales force for you, then you will need to educate them as to how to spot a potential client, how much you value them doing this for you, and what to do next. Go back to the previous chapter and look at the Pain Points you solve for your clients. How can your network physically see, hear, taste or even smell that someone needs your services? What are the sorts of comments that you will hear them say?

For example, someone who may be ready to change their accountant will say things like:

- I'm not sure what my accountant actually does to justify what he is charging me.
- My accountant only seems to get in touch with me when he wants his bill paid or it is time for year end.
- I'm unhappy with the current level of service I am receiving from my accountant.
- My business is growing rapidly and I think it may be outgrowing my current accountant.

You also need to educate your network that giving you referrals is a good thing. Do this by saying *Thank you*. You could:

- Send them a handwritten note saying *Thank you*

- Give them a modest gift

- Give them a referral in return

- Buy them lunch or a drink

- Offer them a spotter's fee or commission split for any successful introductions or referrals. Be aware that some professionals may not for ethical or regulatory reasons be able to accept a spotter's fee or commission split.

Your Networking Routine

In this chapter we have talked about how you are going to network your way to success, and started to think about what you are going to do to implement your Networking Strategy. To build your regular Networking Routine identify what you will do daily, weekly and monthly to achieve your networking aims.

DAILY NETWORKING ROUTINE

- ■ Check My 'People To Keep Close To' List And @Mentions On Twitter
- ■ Do my 9 mins daily Linkedin routine

WEEKLY NETWORKING ROUTINE

- ■ Attend fortnightly breakfast meeting
- ■ Add new blog post to Defero Law
- ■ Check prominent legal bloggers and comment on at least one new blog post
- ■ Find 20-30 articles to share on Twitter & Linkedin for the next week

MONTHLY NETWORKING ROUTINE

- ■ Update my relationship plans and plan activity for next 3 months
- ■ Plan my blogging content for next week

Diagram 9.6: Example of a Networking Routine

 Use the Career Kitbag's Networking Routine Planner to help you build a sustainable and effective Networking Routine.

Summary

Building a high quality Referral Network is normally the easiest way to demonstrate a strong Business Case. However to make sure you don't waste time networking, be clear about:

- What is the aim for your Networking Strategy and its activities? How does this link with the Goals in your Partner Track Plan?

- Who do you want to meet and why do you want to meet them?

- What you will do to deepen A-lister relationships in your network to strengthen your Business and Personal Case.

When you are with your contacts, you need to be proactive to help them pass you referrals. Use the SERVICE framework to help them understand the type of referrals you want and need, and how they can help you to gain these referrals.

Action Points

1. Complete your own Network map and identify 3 Actions to add in new relationships where there are gaps. Update your Partner Track Plan with these Actions.

2. Identify at least 3 opportunities to strengthen relationships with contacts who could form the basis of your Referral Networks. Make sure you add in the next steps from your Relationship Plans into your diary.

3. Speak to your best clients and find out where to spend time both physically and on-line. Go and meet 2 potential new A-listers this month. Relegate 4 people from C-list to D-list.

4. Create your own Networking Strategy and build a daily, weekly and monthly Networking Routine.

Further Resources

BOOKS

For help to build your Networking Strategy and generate more business through the relationships in your network, these are great resources:

- *FT Guide To Business Networking: How to use the power of on-line and off-line networking for business success*, Heather Townsend, ISBN 978-1292003955

- *Relationology: 101 Secrets to Grow Your Business Through the Power of Relationships*, Matt Bird, ISBN 978-1783064779

- *Recommended: How to Sell Through Networking and Referrals*, Andy Lopata, ISBN 978-0273757962

- *Never Eat Alone: And Other Secrets to Success, One Relationship at a Time*, Keith Ferrazzi and Tahl Raz, ISBN 978-0385512053

- *The 29% Solution: 52 Weekly Networking Success Strategies*, Ivan R. Misner, ISBN 978-1929774548

WEBSITES

- *Business Networking:* http://www.business-networking.co.uk

- *Relationology* – the art and science of creating relationships: http://www.relationology.co.uk

PART IV

Becoming a member of the club

When your partners admit you to the partnership they are inviting you to become a member of their very exclusive private members club. Before they will do this, you will need to have gained their trust so that they feel that you act and think like them, and can be relied upon to run your part of the firm safely. Your Personal Case for partnership is where you demonstrate how you meet and exceed the standards required for a partner in your firm.

In this part of the book, we consider exactly what you need to do to create and then articulate your Personal Case to your partners. For example:

- The basics of your Personal Case
- How to think and act like a partner

10

Building your Personal Case:

Topics covered in this chapter:

- What is your Personal Case for partnership?
- What tools are available to benchmark your personal suitability for partnership?
- How to create your internal PR campaign to support your recommendation for partner

((Positive thinking will let you use the ability which you have, and that is awesome.

ZIG ZIGLAR

Your partners need to know that you can do more than hit your numbers. They want to know that you also have a strong Personal Case. This chapter investigates what is meant by your Personal Case and how to prepare it.

What is your Personal Case for partnership?

Shouldn't the best candidate for partnership always get to partner? Well, that's not always what happens. It is fairly common to hear about partners sitting around the table, openly acknowledging that a candidate has a very strong Business Case, will credibly lead their part of the firm, and is very likely to make the firm lots of money. But then something is missing. Something doesn't connect for the partners at the table, so they turn the candidate down for partnership. The missing link here is the Personal Case for partnership. Your Personal Case is sometimes talked about as the emotional part of your *overall case* and/or the skills, attitudes and behaviours your firm needs its partners to have. A well-organised firm such as BDO will be agreeing the Business Case for a new partner a few years before it is needed. They then work with the potential candidates to build their Personal Case for partner. By the time new partners are needed in BDO, the partners should have several candidates with strong Personal Cases to choose from.

Your Personal Case is just as important as your Business Case. After all, when you are accepted into the partnership, you are being admitted into a private club – one where typically you can make a large amount of money. No partner wants to introduce someone into the club who will upset the natural order of the club.

It's very difficult to convey in a written Business Case or even an assessment on your skills, attitudes or behaviours, why you truly:

- 'Fit in',
- 'Connect with the partners', and
- Can be relied upon to safely lead the firm in the future.

Ultimately you may be asking some of your partners to trust you with the business that they may have founded or grown over the last 20 to 25 years. Can they trust you to carry on the business and take it into the future? Remember, their capital may be at stake if you muck up!

This is why you need to spend time *before* the formal part of the Partnership Admissions Process strengthening your Personal Case; i.e. by:

- Growing your profile across the partnership
- Lobbying and building your fan base in the partnership
- Running your own internal PR campaign.

The importance of playing to your strengths

There is no such thing as the 'perfect' individual. We all have strengths and weaknesses. Very often our strengths can be over-played and then become a weakness for us. When you become aware of your natural strengths and talents you can improve your performance by choosing work that plays to these strengths, and team members who complement these. The people who have built the strongest Personal Case for partnership have almost always created a ticket for partnership based on their personal strengths.

Case Study: Simon

Simon, an Auditor, gained a reputation for having great accuracy and excelled in technical areas that demanded a good eye for detail. However, he often found it hard to review his jobs within the time allowed, because of his thirst for detail and his tendency to make sure the details were absolutely correct. It was only when he became aware of this core strength becoming a weakness that he was able to correct it. He did this by getting a member of his team to review the audit report for him. He then did a quick final 'once over' of the audit report. This meant he had to spend less time reviewing the job, but his eye for detail was able to pick up mistakes missed by other people.

What tools are available to benchmark your strengths and personal suitability for partnership?

Every firm is different. Different firms will provide different tools for you to benchmark your personal suitability for partnership. Your firm may have nothing or a well-thought out kitbag of tools for you to access.

For example, Allen & Overy and BDO will put their high potential senior associates and directors through a development centre, to help them understand their current suitability for partner before they go through the formal Partnership Admissions Process. If your firm doesn't offer much in the way of help to assess your strengths and weaknesses, there is nothing stopping you acquiring or creating the tools you need.

Psychometric assessments: These are used to measure your aptitude, personal style or ability. Common assessments include leadership skills assessments, your preferences about how you work and communicate, emotional intelligence tests and personality-based assessments. We use a tool called PROPHET by Optima[9] with nearly all of our clients, to help them understand where their strengths are best used within the business cycle.

360-degree feedback: This is where you gain feedback from people you work with, including your immediate line manager, people who work for you and peers. Some firms have very formal annual 360° feedback exercises, which the senior members and/or the whole firm is required to do. Some 360° feedback exercises are tailored to a specific requirement, such assessing your leadership skills.

Competency frameworks and role descriptions: These are documents that detail the standards expected of partners in the firm. For example, Grant Thornton, a Top 5 accountancy firm in the UK, has a very structured and comprehensive competency framework for its partners.

Self-assessment questionnaires: These are questionnaires that help you self-assess to see where you are strong or weak. For example, early in this book was a questionnaire to help you assess the gaps in your Business Case and Personal Case for partnership.

Performance reviews: Most performance reviews will give you a good idea of how you are viewed and how well you are seen to be performing.

---

9   http://www.optimaabr.com/prophet

How to create your internal PR campaign to support your recommendation for partner

When your partners sit around the partnership table and discuss either formally or informally who they would like to make up to partner, how many partners would be pitching you, and 'fighting your corner'? Like a panel-based job interview, you will not be at the table when the final decisions are taken on who should get to partner this time around. This is why you need to have built up a strong fan base within the partnership well before the formal Partnership Admissions Process starts.

If you are an internal candidate for partnership you will benefit from a ready-made fan base. As a minimum you want to have built enough relationships with partners within your firm so that they know who you are, and are ideally positive about you becoming a partner. However, you will need to have more than just your Mentor and Sponsoring Partner raving about you to the other partners. How many advocates you need at the partnership table is not a question that can be answered with any degree of certainty. However, it is suffice to say that a good answer is *the more the merrier*.

 Use the Career Kitbag's 'Guide to creating your internal PR campaign' to help you build a strong fan base amongst the partners in your firm.

How to build your fan base amongst the partnership in your firm

Build up your internal and external market value

Before you can even plan your assault to the partnership table your client work needs to have done some of the talking for you. Your financials need to be strong, and clients need to be saying good things about you; i.e. you need to be in demand both by partners in the firm and clients external to the firm.

Take part in cross-firm initiatives and projects

There are always opportunities to get involved in cross-firm projects outside of your client work. Do choose carefully, and aim to be present on committees, steering groups, projects or assignments where you will get to increase your internal network and contact with key influential partners. Having a presence on cross-firm initiatives, projects or committees should form a part of your personal Networking Strategy.

Talk to partners outside of your department

Gasp, yes – you are going to need to create the time to get to know partners outside of your department. Do take this opportunity to ask them about what the practice needs in its new partners. Find out how they could see you fitting into the partnership and what skills they believe you would need to develop. Get their views on your Business Case and Personal Case. There is no stronger advocate than a partner who feels that they have had a say in your Business Case ...

Avoid having a fixed date in mind when you want to make partner

One of the faux pas that many potential partners make is having a fixed idea of when they want to make partner. Equity partners get incredibly cheesed off hearing that so-and-so has to be a partner by next year. There may be better candidates ahead of you, or the economy is such that there aren't any new partners being admitted for a few years. By all means have an 'ideal timescale' in your head, or a provisional loose timescale that you are publicly working towards. Just don't go around telling partners that you will be a partner by a certain point in time.

Go to firm socials

The firm's socials may not the top of your list for things you want to do. However, they normally give you great access to many of the firm's partners who you would not normally bump into. Take the opportunity to talk to partners you don't know at these events and also organise a one-to-one over breakfast, coffee, lunch or a drink after work.

Take a strong interest in them and their part of the practice

Most people really appreciate being listened too – and partners are no different. In fact, they do tend to have an ego (not all partners), which needs a certain amount of stroking. Almost treat your partners as if they are your best client – after all, they are probably the biggest stakeholder in your career right now.

Choose an influential Mentor

I clearly remember working with the Head of Audit at my old firm. I was amazed how much influence and power this partner yielded. In an ideal world, you want a Mentor with this level of influence and power. These are the people who can easily facilitate your path to partnership and 'sell' you to the other partners. Sometimes just the fact that this influential partner is championing your cause is enough to get a partner to vote for you.

Find referrals for them

There is nothing quite like bringing in high quality referrals for other partners to generate a great fan base for you. Partners love work winners and in particular, work winners who bring in stuff for them personally.

How to use your Mentor and Sponsoring Partner to help strengthen your Personal Case for partnership

In Chapter 3 we talked about having a Mentor and Sponsoring Partner to help you build a cast-iron Business Case and Personal Case for partnership. There are many ways that you can use these two members of your support team.

They can influence on your behalf

Your Mentor and Sponsoring Partner are your eyes and ears at the partnership table. If they do a great job of influencing other partners to support your application for partner, you may find that you have an easier ride through the Partnership Admissions Process. No matter how influential your Mentor and Sponsoring Partner are, it is truly in your own personal interest to prepare diligently for the Partnership Admissions Process, as you never know what may happen.

Case Study: Roseanne

Roseanne was an ex-Big 4 partner who had applied for a partner role in a mid-tier firm. Her Sponsoring Partner had done a great PR campaign and influenced the firm's partners about the need for her Business Case and why she was the right candidate for the role. As a consequence she found that she was asked very little about her Business Case in the interviews.

They can be totally honest with you

All too often difficult conversations don't happen in Professional Service firms. I've been there in a post-Assessment Centre debrief with a Sponsoring Partner and his potential partner, only to find the Sponsoring Partner say to me,

> We didn't think he would get through as he was rated 3 (performing as expected) in his current role.

As you can expect this potential partner had crashed and burned at the Assessment Centre. His performance at the Assessment Centre effectively spelled the end of his career at the firm, and he was made redundant less than 12 months later. Your Sponsoring Partner, unlike this potential partner's sponsor, should be the one to have the difficult conversation to tell you why you are not ready to go for partner this time around. Having an honest and critical friend in the form of your

Mentor or Sponsoring Partner is vital to help you truly understand your strengths and weaknesses, plus whether you are ready for Partner Track. It is better to have someone honestly tell you that you are not ready – or may not ever be ready – than put yourself through a tough ordeal and handle with the damage to your self-esteem and confidence afterwards. If they think you may never be ready you may be able to negotiate with them tangible support, such as time off for interviews or career coaching to help you exit and find the right firm or role for you.

As well as telling you whether you are ready or not, what they can also do is give you good guidance about how to sell yourself to the partnership in a way which will help them want you as part of the club.

If you are not getting this level of insight from your Mentor *and* Sponsoring Partner, then you need to be asking them these sorts of detailed questions.

They can help you use the right phrases to get backing from the partners

Your Sponsoring Partner is putting their reputation on the line when they recommend you for partner; i.e. they, personally, have a vested interest in helping you get to partner. Therefore, make sure you tap into their expertise to ensure that you have added the correct phrases and 'hot buttons' to your Business Case and Personal Case, which will make the other partners consider you a good choice for partner.

They can connect you to the key influencers in the partnership

Your Mentor and Sponsoring Partner should be able to introduce you to the key partners who you need to get on side to make you a sure bet for partnership. They can also tell you who the partners you can safely avoid because they hold little or no influence or that you need to avoid at all costs.

Summary

Your Personal Case for partner is where you demonstrate that you think, act and feel at the standard expected of a partner. Sometimes this is assessed formally within the Partnership Admissions Process. However, it is difficult to often convey in a written assessment why you can be trusted to lead the firm into the future and fit in nicely around the partnership table. Therefore, when you are on Partner Track, part of the work you need to do is build your own fan base amongst the partners.

Action Points

1. Find out if there is a role description or competency framework for partners at your firm. If there is, measure yourself against the standards expected of partners. How well do you match up? What can you do to develop yourself? Add any action points to your Partner Track Plan.

2. Seek out tools that will help you assess your strengths and weaknesses. Use these tools to help you understand your current suitability for partnership. Where can you use your strengths to build a strong Personal Case for partnership?

3. Consult with your Mentor and Sponsoring Partner to form a convincing argument to demonstrate why your firm needs your skill set, knowledge, thinking or decision-making style within the partnership.

4. Start to construct your own internal PR campaign to support your recommendation for partnership. Within your campaign identify ways that you can build your profile and fan base with parts of the practice that you don't normally spend time with. Add your actions to your Partner Track Plan.

5. Diarise the next few firm social events. Organise your work and home life so that you can attend these.

6. Instead of picking up the phone to people in the same building, start walking over to see them.

7. Ask your Mentor and Sponsoring Partner to identify which partners hold the most informal and formal influence around the partnership table. Seek their advice for how to get these people to become advocates of yours.

Further resources

BOOKS

These books will help you discover more of your strengths and how to use these to your advantage within your firm:

- *Now, Discover Your Strengths: How to Develop Your Talents and Those of the People You Manage*, Marcus Buckingham and Donald O. Clifton, ISBN 978-1416502654

- *What Got You Here Won't Get You There: How successful people become even more successful*, Marshall Goldsmith, ISBN 978-1781250204

- *Nice Girls Don't Get the Corner Office: Unconscious Mistakes Women Make That Sabotage Their Careers*, Lois P. Frankel, ISBN 978-1455558896

11

How to think and act like a partner

Topics covered in this chapter:

- How to be seen as a member of 'the club'
- How to have more gravitas and 'executive presence'
- How to build and develop a team
- What motivates people
- How to deliver feedback to your team
- Setting goals and objectives

❝ *The key is to keep company only with people who uplift you, whose presence calls forth your best.*

EPICTETUS

The best Personal Case you can have is if you are already seen by your partners as 'one of us'. This means thinking and acting as if you are already a partner. This chapter explores how you can do this by being seen as a member of 'the club', having gravitas and developing and building your own team.

How to be seen as a member of 'the club'

I was recently talking to a senior partner in a London city law firm. He told me that when he was on Partner Track he lived in fear of annoying partners in his firm. (He actually used stronger language than that!) To be seen as a member of 'the club' you need to be respected and liked by the partners in your firm. It may seem very unfair, but if one partner decides that they don't like you then your partnership prospects are radically reduced.

One of the best ways of being seen as 'one of us' is to build your profile within the junior partner population and the people who are likely to make partner before you. Then as they progress further up the partnership ladder, they can take you with them.

In many ways, your partners need to see you as an equal, or very nearly an equal before they will let you into their club. The easiest way to do this is change the type of conversations you are having with the partners and your team. For example:

- Do you consider the firm's agenda alongside your own agenda?
- Are you thinking beyond your own caseload or assignments to what really matters to the firm and other partners?
- Do you think commercially and strategically?
- How can you get involved in business development initiatives?
- How can you generate new business for other partners in the firm?

Within any firm will be influential groups of partners as well as individuals who wield much more power than their title, status or responsibilities suggest. Part of your remit when on Partner Track is to understand who these partners are and the political sensitivities of the partnership. At this stage in your career it is less about your technical excellence and more about who you know and how they view you.

Think like a partner

In Chapter 4 we identified the various aspects of the role of a modern day partner. It may be unrealistic to do all of these before you actually get the role of partner, however the more you can show that you are thinking as if you are a partner, the stronger your Personal Case will be. For example:

- Are you helping others in your team develop?

© HEATHER TOWNSEND

- Do you and your team hit your billing and collection targets?

- Do you demonstrate by what you say and do that you are committed to the firm's strategy?

- Are you hungry for more leadership and management responsibility?

- Have you found ways to be more involved in the leadership and management of your part of the practice?

- Do the partners in your part of the practice regularly consult your opinion?

How to have more gravitas and executive presence

One of the common questions asked by senior associates and directors, is how to have the level of gravitas and executive presence normally associated with partners. Here are the factors that can help you.

Posture and body language

Probably one of the biggest drivers of gravitas and executive presence is how you hold yourself, and the body language that you use – whether consciously or sub-consciously. Make sure you sit up straight, don't hunch your shoulders forward, and try to elongate your spine, but keep your shoulders down. In pilates you are encouraged to imagine that someone has a piece of string on your head and is pulling you up. However, make sure your shoulders stay down!

So much of what people call gravitas is actually their reaction to the other person's body language. Every so often take stock of your body language and see whether you are projecting an outward confidence with your body language.

Language

The next biggest impact on your gravitas is the language that you use. Not just how you say the words, but the words that you actually use. When you are talking are you using words that demonstrate your passion? When you are truly passionate about a subject, it can convey gravitas, as long as you don't let your emotions run away with you.

For example, *"I like doing SAP implementations"* vs. *"I get a real buzz out of helping large businesses to configure SAP to work for them, in way which gives them real control over the numbers and performance."*

When your self-belief, rather than lack of it, comes through the words you use, this can ramp up your gravitas. Do watch out for weasel words, umms/errs, self-effacing words or hesitancy, as this will reduce your gravitas. Have you noticed that some people will carefully select their words and tend to avoid using 30 words when just 10 will do. Think about the great orators such as Barack Obama, Winston Churchill, Martin Luther King and Gandhi who have honed and crafted their famous speeches. Each word has been carefully chosen.

Pace your words

When you think of folks with gravitas, they never speak quickly. Take a look at Obama's inauguration speech. This is a man who is completely at the top of his game and is the poster boy for gravitas in this speech. He doesn't hurry his speech and takes his time over his words. Although he is using an autocue, he uses pauses for impact. Now you may not be presenting to an audience, but next time you need to up your gravitas take your time over what you are going to say. Make eye contact with people you need to influence, even if you are just one-on-one with a partner and add in pauses to emphasise key words or phrases.

Inner belief

If you don't have belief or confidence in yourself then this will leak out through your body language, words and voice. Therefore, an important factor in having gravitas is to really believe in yourself, your abilities, your self-worth, your subject and what you are saying.

Dress for the image you want to portray

Executive presence includes looking the part. For example, if you are a woman, having your hair pulled back off your face may give you more gravitas.

Emphasise key words

Sometimes when people are softly spoken this can impact their gravitas. Whilst there is nothing wrong, per se, with being softly spoken, if you want to have greater presence, you may find you need to raise your voice a little and put some subtle emphasis on key words and phrases.

How to create your team

All of us perform better and more willingly when we know why we're doing what we have been told or asked to do.

ZIG ZIGLAR

Most partnerships are looking for their new partners to be people who they can trust to run the firm. This means you need to be a triple threat; i.e. someone who can win work, be excellent with clients and develop a team beneath you. In fact, people may be turned down for partner because they have either neglected to develop their successor or their team had limited respect for them. In other words, the quality of the team you build, and how the other non-partners view you are just as important as the quality of your client portfolio.

One of the only ways you may be able to create the time to build your client portfolio is to create a strong team beneath and around you to service the client work you win.

To create your strong team, you need to be prepared to play any number of roles as a team leader:

Route finder and target setter: The team will be looking to you to set their purpose and targets, and help them identify the plan to help achieve these. Ideally your targets and the team's targets will be aligned and flow from the firm or departmental overall strategy.

Facilitator: It takes time and energy to get a team to work well together. Your role will be to work within the team to help the team bond and trust each other. There will always be roadblocks along the way, and it is your role to help remove these to enable the team to deliver.

Coach and trainer: You can't expect all your team members, particularly the more junior members to have the right skills and behaviours to do the job you need them to do. Your role is to act as the team coach as well as coach to team members, to help them develop and behaviour at the level expected of them.

Motivator: Your team will be looking to you to help provide the motivation for the team as a whole, but also on an individual level. This means that you need to work out what makes each individual team member tick, and how you can help motivate them. Very often, professionals in practice are motivated by interesting work, career progression and feeling valued for who they are and what they bring to the team/firm.

Conflict resolver: You can say with some degree of certainty that your role as a team leader will involve resolving conflict. This could be individual team member disputes through to other people wanting to reallocate your resource to their assignment. It is not unusual for a team to go through a phase characterised by conflict. It often occurs after the team has initially formed and gone through the 'honeymoon' stage. It is your role to resolve these conflicts as and when they appear, and if possible nip them in the bud before they become serious or entrenched.

How to give feedback successfully

As the saying goes, "feedback is the breakfast of champions". It is also the best way to help your team members develop and perform at the level required. However, feedback given incorrectly or thoughtlessly can often do more harm than good. I'm sure we can all recall occasions when we've been hurt by feedback given in an insensitive way.

What makes good quality feedback:

- It is actionable
- It helps the receiver understand exactly what they did and the impact on others
- Timely
- Delivered in a way which achieves the desired result
- It is grounded in fact and observation rather than hearsay or conjecture
- It is given when emotions have died down and people are calm.

There are many models or processes around of how to give feedback to someone. My preferred model is the Situation Behaviour Outcome (SBO) feedback model.

What is SBO?

The SBO model is a feedback model which can be used to deliver both positive and constructive feedback.

The SBO model:

Situation   Describe where and when the observed behaviour occurred, and what happened. Remember to be specific.

Behaviour   Describe what you saw or heard. Avoid interpretations and judgements such as, 'You weren't listening to me.' Rather describe the person's *behaviour*: 'When I was talking, you pushed your chair away from the table and gazed out of the window.'

Outcome   Share with the individual the outcome or impact of the behaviour on you and/or on others. Outcome is what you or others experienced. It can include work outcomes, client satisfaction, work team and/or the larger firm. Most often, it starts with 'I felt ...' or 'I was ...' or 'It appeared to me that others were ...'

Some examples of using SBO feedback:

Weak feedback: Jane, the new client meeting went well today – thanks.

Effective feedback: Jane, at the new client meeting this afternoon [Situation] *you listened really well and showed the client that you understood* [Behaviour]. *As a result I could clearly see rapport building and the client trusting you more as the meeting went on* [Outcome]. *I think we may win this client based on how you handled the meeting*

Summary

Your route to having a strong Personal Case is intrinsically linked to your ability to think and act like a partner. This means you need to be seen by your partners as *one of us* and successfully lead, manage and develop your team. Building a successful team around you will free you from client work and enable you to focus on building a strong Business Case by growing your client portfolio and practice as a whole.

Action Points

1. Have a private conversation with each of your team members or more junior members of your department, to find out what they like about their role and where they would like to progress their career.

2. Ask three people you trust and work with regularly for feedback on your abilities as a team leader. What will you do to act on their feedback to improve your abilities as a team leader?

3. If you supervise or have line management responsibilities for people in your department, diarise regular conversations with your team members to find out how they are doing and what progress they are making on their career aims and current client assignments.

4. Book some time in with your Mentor and ask them how they learnt to manage people and lead teams. Then take action on what you have learnt.

5. If you are employed within a firm, ask a member of your firm, such as a member of the HR team, to sit in on a performance review that you run, to give you feedback and suggestions of what you could have done differently to be more effective.

6. Think about the teams you are either a member of or lead. What stage of team development are they at? What three actions will you do to increase the performance of each team?

7. Work with a coach to help improve your people management and leadership skills.

8. Volunteer to mentor a more junior member of your firm.

Further resources

BOOKS

These are highly recommended books to help you motivate, develop and lead your team:

- *Drive: The Surprising Truth About What Motivates Us*, Daniel H. Pink, ISBN 978-1847677693

- *When Professionals Have to Lead: A New Model for High Performance*, Thomas J. Delong and John J. Gabarro, ISBN 978-1422117378

- *A Practical Guide to Mentoring: How to help others achieve their goals*, David Kay and Roger Hinds, ISBN 978-1845283704

- *Leadership and the One Minute Manager*, Kenneth Blanchard and Patricia Zigarmi, ISBN 978-0007103416

- *Coaching for Performance: GROWing human potential and purpose – the principles and practice of coaching and leadership*, John Whitmore, ISBN 978-1957885354

- *What to Do When You Become the Boss: How New Managers Become Successful Managers*, Bob Selden, ISBN 978-0755361625

WEBSITES

- How to make partner: http://howtomakepartner.com/category/managing-others/

PART V

The final stages of partner track

You are now coming to the final stages of your long journey to become a partner. If you have taken the time over the last few years to build a cast-iron Business Case and Personal Case for partner, then these stages should hold no fear for you.

In this part of the book, we explore:

- How to shine when you are going through the Partnership Admissions Process
- What to do after the Partnership Vote

12

How to shine as you go through the partnership admissions process

Topics covered in this chapter:

- What is the purpose of the Partnership Admissions Process
- What to expect at a Partner Assessment Centre
- How to prepare for verbal, numerical and logical reasoning tests
- How to shine in your pitch for partnership in the Partner Panel Interview
- Strategies to perform strongly in a competency-based interview

❝ Tough times never last, but tough people do.

ROBERT H. SCHULLER

If you have spent the time creating a cast-iron Business Case and Personal Case for partnership, then you should have nothing to fear in the Partnership Admissions Process. There are many big firms, including Big 4 and Magic Circle firms, who now start preparing their high flyers for partnership a good 1–3 years before they put them through the Partnership Admissions Process. This is to give their high flyers the time to create a strong Business Case and Personal Case for partner.

Regardless of the strength of your Business Case and Personal Case you can still blow it as you go through the Partnership Admissions Process by not preparing well enough. This chapter will cover what you can expect and strategies to help you be at your best as you progress.

Why do firms have a Partnership Admissions Process?

Every firm has a different Partnership Admissions Process. Even if your firm does not have a publically stated formal or informal process, your partners will still go through a similar set of decisions and discussions every time they admit a new member to the partnership. You may find that some of the process is documented in the Partnership Agreement.

Probably the biggest mistake that any potential partner makes is to consider the Partnership Admissions Process as a long drawn-out job interview or panel for promotion. It is actually a process by which the partners in your firm decide who is the best candidate to be trusted with the leadership and commercial responsibilities of becoming a business owner: in other words, your current and future suitability for the partner role. Giving equity to a new person is normally not a spur of the moment decision, which is why deciding is a long drawn-out and detailed process. After all they want to make sure that anyone who owns equity in their business is:

- Committed to the long-term vision of the business
- A positive influence on the other equity holders within the business
- Willing to put the interests of the business above any personal agendas or personal short-term interests
- Going to strengthen the decision-making ability of the practice area's leadership team
- Going to help the partnership be greater than the sum of its parts
- Someone who thinks and behaves collegiately
- Certain to be around for the long term
- Prepared to invest in leaving a legacy within the business
- Willing to help the partnership become more robust and sustainable

- Willing to more than pull their weight commercially; i.e. will increase the size of the pie for the rest of the partnership.

Consequently, all of these factors, not just the respective merit of your Business Case and Personal Case, will influence the partners' decision about whether to admit you to the partnership. Some firms can take 6–9 months to put their people through the Partnership Admissions Process. The last stage is always a formal Partnership Vote by the partners.

The typical Partnership Admissions Process

Most mid- to large-sized firms have a Partnership Selection Committee, normally supported by the HR director, who are responsible for managing the selection process for the firm. In small firms new partners may not be admitted every year. When a firm is going through a particularly lean period they may take a decision not to admit any new partners until the firm is in a better financial position.

Usually, the selection process is as follows:

1. Determine the size of the firm's partner pool. The firm's Management Board will decide, based on submissions by heads of practice areas, how many new partners are strategically and financially viable.

2. Identification of suitable candidates for promotion to partner. Partners will sponsor people within their department who they are believe are ready to be admitted to the partnership. In the majority of mid- to large-sized firms, potential partners will know at least 1–3 years ahead when they will be eligible for partnership consideration.

3. Each candidate will have a Partnership Nomination Pack. Their Sponsoring Partner, the candidate and sometimes the head of their practice area normally prepare these. At this stage in some firms, potential partner candidates may be required to attend an Assessment Centre (see below), following which a report on each candidate will be prepared by the Partner Selection Committee.

The contents of a Partnership Nomination Pack will normally include some or all of the following:

- Their Business Case

- A self-assessment

- Report on their financial performance

- Their performance and development reviews for the last three years

- Psychometric assessment reports

- Any reports from assessment and development centres, in particular if they have attended a Partner Assessment Centre (see later for more details)

- The Head of Department and Sponsoring Partner's business and financial case reports

- Feedback from clients and internal feedback

- The Management Board recommendations for the candidate.

4. The Partner Selection Committee will then interview the candidate, their Head of Department, and sometimes their Sponsoring Partner. There could be as many as 6 interviews per candidate. Candidates, particularly if they are external to the firm, may be asked to complete verbal and numerical reasoning tests.

5. The Partner Selection Committee will then discuss the candidates, and make their recommendations for the firm's Management Board to approve. In most firms, the equity partners then vote to approve each new partner.

What will the Partner Selection Committee be thinking about as they discuss each candidate?

Members of the Partnership Selection Committee are entrusted with deciding which candidates are put through to the Partnership Vote, so their own reputations are on the line. The last thing they want to personally do is recommend someone for partnership who then either:

- Doesn't get through the Partnership Vote
- Fails to achieve their Business Case
- Becomes a nightmare to work with around the partnership table
- Leaves within a few years of being admitted to the partnership

Accordingly, they will be considering the potential reasons why they *shouldn't* admit each candidate to partnership. For example, they will be thinking:

- Can I work with this candidate personally?
- Will other highly influential partners work with them well?
- Am I comfortable letting them know all the inner secrets of the partnership?
- Can the candidate be trusted to know the dirty laundry of the partnership?
- Will the most influential partners back them in the vote?
- Do I believe in the viability of their Business Case?

Very often these set of questions, which are not included within the Partnership Nomination Packs, will massively influence whether or not the candidate gets put forward for the Partnership Vote.

The Partner Assessment Centre

The Partner Assessment Centre is normally only one part of the Partnership Admission Process. The purpose of the centre is to help your firm gain insight into your suitability for partner, particularly your leadership skill set. The preparation you need to do is normally fairly minor. Familiarise yourself with the firm's competency framework so you know what the assessors will be looking for, and aim to arrive refreshed after a good night's sleep.

What happens in a Partner Assessment Centre?

An Assessment Centre normally lasts between 1–3 days. Almost without exception, they are intensive and incredibly tiring. Expect to tumble into bed after a day at the centre absolutely shattered. Most centres involve you participating in a number of exercises based around real-life situations, and some one-to-one interviews. After you leave the centre, the assessors will then get together and review the individuals' performances. They will normally then make recommendations on who is ready for partnership and what an individual needs to improve on to be ready for partnership.

The exercises

The exercises you complete are normally a mixture of individual and group work, role-plays or written work. It is quite common for real life business scenarios to form the context for the exercises you do. As you would expect these exercises will test your responses to see whether you are thinking like a business owner of the firm. The challenges you will be grappling with may involve external clients, internal people, strategic and tactical issues across the full range of firm functions.

Many centres use a traffic light system to rate attendees' performance in an exercise; i.e.

> *Red = performed significantly under the level expected for a junior partner*
>
> *Amber = some small improvement needed to perform at the level of a junior partner*
>
> *Green = performed at or above the level expected for a junior partner.*

As you are taking part in a whole series of exercises, don't worry too much if you think you have performed badly in one exercise. These centres are designed so that each partner competency can be assessed in more than one exercise. Your performance will be evaluated on how you did across the whole of the exercises, rather than just on one exercise.

Despite how it may come across, you are not competing against the other people on the centre. A well-run centre will evaluate individuals on their own performance rather than how others perform on the day. Sometimes a firm will use actors or partners from the firm to bring an element of realism to the exercises. When you are doing the exercises aim to be yourself and use your knowledge and experience to handle the situations you are exposed to. With all these things most exercises are constructed so that there isn't one right answer.

It can be tempting to dismiss the imaginary situations or assume you know what the assessors are looking for. This can be dangerous and it is best to be positive about the process and give it your best shot. Do get involved in the exercises as the assessors can only use the evidence that they see or hear on the day.

Competency-based Interview

Very often within the centre you will have a competency-based interview that lasts up to an hour with an assessor. The assessor will ask you for very detailed examples of actual projects or pieces of work that you have done. The assessor will use probing questions about these examples to help them understand your style and approach in dealing with work situations that partners may have to cope with.

Feedback on your performance

You will receive feedback so expect to be debriefed by your assessor or Sponsoring Partner. This could be on the last day of the centre or at a later date. Your debrief will include feedback on your strengths and development needs against your firm's competencies. The assessor's report recommending whether you should be advanced for admission to the partnership will be given to the firm's Management Board and the Partner Selection Committee.

Verbal and numerical reasoning tests

Lateral hires at partner level, and very occasionally internal candidates for partner, may be required to complete verbal and numerical reasoning tests. These are normally nothing to be feared. However, they can seem to be daunting if you haven't done any of these tests for a fair few years. As with all these things, the more you practise and the more you gain confidence at these tests, the easier they will become.

Here are some tips based on a recent client's experience of doing verbal and numerical reasoning tests on how to complete them without stress.

Relax – you are bright and able

Remember that to get to the top of the professions means that you are pretty astute and bright. You are perfectly able to fly through these tests.

Do some practice tests but cut down the time you have to do them

As with all these things, practice makes perfect. Your firm or prospective firm should be able to point you in the direction of some practice tests. When you do these, cut down the amount of time you have to do them. This will raise the stakes whilst you are doing the practice tests. Then when it comes to the actual test you will find it far easier and less stressful because you have more time to do them.

Decide when and where you will take the test

Very often tests are delivered and administered on-line. This means you can do them anywhere there is an internet connection. Normally they are to be completed at a time that is convenient for you. The days of having to be in a room to complete psychometric tests are probably numbered now. Therefore, decide on the best time of day for you to take them. Are you more alert in the morning? Or in the evening? When can you get peace and quiet to concentrate?

Read the questions carefully

Before you start doing the test check carefully how it will be administered. How many answers do you need to give to a question?

Can you go back to any question you haven't answered? Do take your time to properly read each question.

The Partner Panel Interviews

Most firms will put all their candidates through a gruelling series of interviews. The interviews are likely to include a competency-based interview, a 'risk and quality' interview and a Partner Panel Interview.

Within your interviews your partners are, of course, assessing the strength of your Business Case and Personal Case. They are also looking for some specifics. For example, they are looking to see whether you can demonstrate a business owner mindset. If you are in a Big 4 firm or large international firm, the interviewers will be testing the strength of your global and commercial mindset. You can expect to be tested on your awareness of specific issues facing your firm. You will be expected to have heard about the issues and have a point of view about them.

Another specific that the interviewers will be looking for is robust evidence of how you have built up strong relationships. Many people in the interviews will talk about relationships, but will struggle to articulate evidence that the relationships they have built will bring in commercial opportunities for the firm. You will need to show:

- Who knows you in your marketplace?
- How have you raised your profile there?
- Which clients would follow you if you left the firm?
- Who contacts you to pick your brains?
- Which partners and professional intermediaries consider you the Go-To Expert?
- What relationships you are building and how are you consistently and sustainably strengthening your Referral Network.
- The number and value of referrals your Referral Network has given you, whether or not you service the work.

- How resilient your Business Case is; i.e. what would happen if your main client went bust or the market changed significantly?

Your interviews are not just evaluating what will happen if they make you partner now. They are considering what will happen a few years down the line.

As you would expect your interviewers will be assessing whether you already are acting and thinking like a partner in your firm. They will want to find out whether you are mentally, personally and professionally committed to making partner. It is not unusual for people in the Big 4 to make partner at the *second* time of asking, because they've strengthened their Business Case and Personal Case plus demonstrated they have the resilience and stamina to go through the Partnership Admissions Process again.

To help you prepare for these interviews, have a go at answering these questions:

- How would you describe what you do and your marketplace in less than one minute?

- Talk me through specifically how have you have helped your department's development and growth?

- What have you done personally to help your part of the firm become more profitable, and reduce WIP and Lockup?

- How have you personally demonstrated that you are a role model for the firm's values?

- In relation to the standards partners are expected to achieve, explain how you are meeting these already?

- If you are admitted to the partnership, what will it help you do that being a senior associate couldn't?

- What have you had to give up to realise your ambition of making partner?

- What do you think are the key trends, issues and challenges that the leadership team should be dealing with right now?

- Given the current trends in the marketplace, what do you think the future direction of the firm should be?

- If you are admitted to the partnership, what will you have achieved five years from now?

- What would be the impact on your practice size if your top 2 clients or referrers stopped sending you work?

- What do you see as the biggest risks to your achieving the numbers, specifically your revenue growth, as set out in you business case?

- What support or guidance will you need to achieve your business case?

- Why should we admit you to the partnership rather than any of the other senior associates going for partnership this year?

- What do you want your legacy to the firm to be?

- Why shouldn't we admit you to the partnership?

The 'risk and quality' interview

Not every firm will put their candidates through this interview. However, expect to have a risk and quality interview if you are being recruited into the firm at partner level. Your technical competence will be assessed in this interview by one of the firm's technical specialists.

Competency-based interviews

Many firms will have codified the technical skills, mindset and behaviours that they need from the partners into a competency framework. It is the competencies within this framework that your competency-based interview will be verifying.

How will you know if you are going to have a competency-based interview?

There is no guarantee that you will have this type of interview. However, if any of these are present, then there is a strong likelihood that some of your interviews will be competency based:

- The firm has a competency framework which covers the partners and you have been given a copy of this
- You have been asked to fill in an application form which asks for 'Evidence of times when you have ...'
- You have got multiple interviews to complete as part of the process
- HR is involved in the interviewing process
- The questions you are being asked within the interview often start with 'Tell me about a time when you ...'

What if you can't evidence everything within the competency framework?

It all depends on what stage in your career you are at. For example, if you were similar to our client who was an ex-Big 4 partner and moving to a senior partner role in a UK Top 6 firm, then you would be expected to pretty much evidence everything within the framework. If you are a director in a Big 4 firm and, therefore not yet senior enough to solely source and win multi-million pound deals, then you wouldn't be expected to evidence everything.

As with all these things, there tends to be points allocated to each question. If you fully satisfy the criteria you will get, for example, 4 points. If you show no evidence at all, you will get 0 points. If you satisfy most of the criteria it will be 3 points. You get the picture. At the end of the interview, your points will be totted up. Very often if your score is above a certain amount you are given a 'green light'. Or you could be given a red light if you have completely failed, and an amber light if you are not quite good enough to pass, but not bad enough to fail.

Tips for passing your competency-based interviews

Here are some tips compiled from people who have gone through a series of very structured competency-based interviews.

Look at your competency framework and identify what evidence you need to demonstrate

Basically, if you want to know what questions you are going to be asked, just look at the competency framework. For example, if it says something like: *demonstrates an ability to win work for the firm* you can expect a question about how you have in the past gone about winning work.

Write down examples and stories you can use in the interview

Go through each of the competencies in the competency framework and think about how you can evidence technical skills, mindset and behaviours for each of them. Then write down the evidence in the form of succinct stories. Transfer these stories to a sheet of paper and take this along to your interview to use as a prompt. Each story needs to contain the impact/results you generated, your role in producing the impact, and a short context of the problem or background.

Write down the questions you may be asked and practice answering them

Go through the competency framework and for each competency and area you are expected to demonstrate, write down a question which will do that. Then ask your Mentor, Sponsoring Partner or supportive friend to ask you each question and you practise answering them. Then get feedback from them on how succinctly you answered the question and how well you evidenced the question.

Take your crib sheet of stories into the interview

If you have this with you in the interview, you can literally tick off the stories as you use and tell them. The crib sheet will help remind you of the key points you want to make in the interview. It can also save your bacon if your mind goes blank when you are asked a question. At the end of the interview, do check to see whether you have ticked off all your stories. If you find that you have not used all your stories, take the opportunity at the end of the interview to talk the interviewers through the evidence you didn't give them. Normally this will happen when the interviewer asks you:

- Do you have any questions for us?
- Is there anything you haven't told us that you think it would be useful for us to know?

Use your Mentor and/or Sponsoring Partner to help you practise for the interview

The last thing you want to do is have your mind go blank during the interview. This is a very real threat! The more time you take to practice your answers to potential questions the less chance that your mind goes blank.

Case Study:
Paul

Paul was going for a new partner role in a Big 4 firm. He devoted a large proportion of time with his Sponsoring Partner to go over his answers to potential interview questions. This helped him be succinct, relaxed and stopped him waffling or going off topic. It also helped him hone his answers to questions so he was making sure he was hitting all the right buttons to get a high score for his competency-based interview.

The Partner Panel Interview

In most mid- to large-sized firms candidates can expect to have a Partner Panel Interview. The Partnership Selection Committee or your firm's Management Board normally makes up the panel.

This interview often takes the form of the candidate pitching their Business Case and Personal Case to the panel, followed by a question and answer session.

How to pitch your Business Case and Personal Case

In Chapter 7 there was a 6-step process to help you communicate your Business Case in a powerful but succinct way. This process can be used to help you turn your Business Case and Personal Case into a pitch. If you use this process you will have whittled your Business Case and Personal Case down to 5–10 slides. The headlines of your slides will tell the 'chapters' of your case. The order of your slides will look something like this:

1. 3-sentence pitch
2. Reason 1 which supports/qualifies 3-sentence pitch
3. Reason 2 which supports/qualifies 3-sentence pitch
4. Reason 3 which supports/qualifies 3-sentence pitch
5. ... and so on ...
6. Risk of not promoting me to partner this time.

Tips on pitching your Business Case and Personal Case to the panel

Keep your cool

Easier said than done – particularly if partnership is riding on this presentation. Nerves can sometimes be good, but can also lead to you drying up, sweating excessively, going red, stumbling over words or even becoming breathless. A couple of deep and long breaths before you start your presentation always helps. If at any point you feel the nerves getting the better of you, stop, take a sip of water and some deep breaths, then carry on.

Envisage the worse case scenarios

Think of what could go wrong in this presentation. Projector break down? Have you got a couple of paper copies of your slides? Drying up? Use cue cards.

Practice, practice, practice

As the phrase goes, practice makes perfect. Ask your Mentor and Sponsoring Partner to be your audience and give you real feedback. Can you record yourself using your smartphone? When you play it back, what do you notice? What could you improve on? Send a copy of the recording of your presentation to your External Coach. They will be able to give you insightful feedback as to how you can improve.

Practice the first and last 3 minutes of your pitch aloud at least ten times. This will 'fix' the words in your head, so that however nervous you may be, you deliver the most important parts of your presentation well.

Plan how long you will take

You will probably have been given a guide as to how long your presentation needs to be. When you do your presentation for real your nerves may make you talk faster – and you get through quicker. When you video yourself time how long it takes. If it's too long, what can you chop out?

Visit the room where you will do the presentation

Do visit the place where you will present before you actually present. Can you take the opportunity to actually practice in the room? Will there be lots of people in the room, and where will they sit? Now think about lines of sight and where you need to stand so you can be easily seen and heard.

Anticipate questions

You can expect to have a question and answer session at the end. This is your chance to really engage the panel in your pitch. Do spend some time thinking of the questions you will may be asked, as these may be the classic difficult interview questions:

- Why should we promote you to partner over some of the other candidates?
- If we could only promote one partner this year, why should it be you?
- If we could only promote one partner this year, why should it *not* be you?
- What weaknesses in the partnership will you strengthen by being promoted to partner?
- What will cause you to fail as a partner?
- What would your team say your greatest weakness is?

Remember that in the question and answer session the partners are not looking for you to repeat what you said, but want to hear the logic or problem-solving process you used to come to your conclusion. If the partners still don't like your argument then check to see whether you have been misunderstood and if necessary clarify. Don't argue for argument's sake – *even if you are a lawyer* – but if you are not convincing the partners, then agree to disagree. Now is not the time to score cheap points ...

Get your Mentor's advice

Your Mentor may even be on the panel you are presenting to. Ask them for tips on what you should say and do in your presentation. Ask them to help you rehearse your presentation and ask them to give you feedback.

Work out if any partner particularly bothers you

Let's be honest, some partners can make anyone feel uncomfortable. If you know that your nemesis is going to be on the panel, take some time to work out what it is that bothers you about them. How could you normalise this reaction? Could you reframe how you react to them? At the end of the day, aim to not take anything from the partner that bothers you personally – they are there to do a job on behalf of the partnership – and may have been asked to play bad cop.

Get to know more of the partners before the presentation

Getting to partner is as much about how many advocates you have in the partnership as it is about your Business Case. Before the presentation spend time with partners in and out of your department, and get their thoughts on your Business Case and Personal Case. Ask them what you should highlight in your presentation and what skills they think you bring that the partnership needs.

 Use the Career Kitbag's 'Guide to designing and delivering impactful presentations' to help you 'wow' your audience in the Partnership Panel Interview.

Final Stage

After each candidate has completed all the different stages of the Partnership Admissions Process, your firm's Management Board and Partnership Selection Committee will recommend who should be promoted to partner. The partners will then all vote on the recommendations. Typically, your Sponsoring Partner will then let you know the result of the vote.

Summary

The Partnership Admissions Process is where the firm fully tests out the strength of your Business Case and Personal Case for partnership. Each firm will have its own process but you can expect to have a series of interviews and potentially an Assessment Centre. It is likely that in one of the interviews you will need to pitch your Business Case to a panel of partners.

The best way to shine through the Partnership Admissions Process is to have already built up a strong Business Case and Personal Case, and to have prepared thoroughly for each part of the process. The last stage of the process is where the partners vote for who they will admit to the partnership this time around.

Action Points

1. Ask your Mentor and Sponsoring Partner what the Partnership Admissions Process is for your firm. Diarise key dates in the process.

2. Take your Business Case and use the process in Chapter 7 to translate your case into a pitch.

3. Have a go at answering the potential interview questions that are detailed in this chapter.

4. If you are required to do verbal and numerical reasoning tests find some practice tests so you know what to expect.

5. Ask your Mentor and Sponsoring Partner to give you interview practice to help you prepare for your interviews.

6. Do your homework on the people who will be interviewing you during the Partnership Admissions Process. What are they interested in? What are their 'hot buttons'?

Further resources

BOOKS

These books will all help you hone your skills in the various stages of your firm's Partnership Admissions Process.

- *How to Pass Numerical Reasoning Tests*, Heidi Smith, ISBN 978-0749467975

- *How to Pass Advanced Verbal Reasoning Tests*, Mike Bryon, ISBN 978-0749467937

- *The Interview Question & Answer Book: Your Definitive Guide to the Best Answers to Even the Toughest Interview Questions*, James Innes, ISBN 978-0273763710

- *Presentation Skills for Quivering Wrecks*, Bob Etherington, ISBN 978-1904879800

13

What happens after the Partnership Vote?

Topics covered in this chapter:

- Your top priorities if you are successful in the vote
- How to pick yourself up if you are unsuccessful in the vote

" Sometimes it's the journey that teaches you a lot about your destination.

DRAKE

Partnership Vote signals the end of Partner Track. Regardless of where you ended up, you have work to do. This chapter explores your immediate next steps after you have heard the results of the vote.

Your top priorities if you are successful in the vote

Firstly, well done for making it to Partner! You have probably made the biggest and toughest step up you are ever going to do in your career. In the few months before your appointment to partner becomes permanent you have some essential activities to do.

Do your due diligence on yourself and your firm

The Partnership Admissions Process is a demanding and exhausting process. Before you formally accept the offer of partnership you need time to recharge and centre yourself. Don't feel as if you have to immediately sign on the dotted line. Do talk with members of your support team, particularly your immediate family and friends, to see about how you and they feel about you finally making it to partner. You may find it very helpful to revisit the due diligence you did in Chapters 5 and 6 of this book. If you have not previously had the right to look at sensitive partnership documents, now is the time to request these documents and finish your due diligence. After all you are going to be investing a chunk of your capital in the firm.

When you sign on the dotted line and accept your new status as a business owner of the firm you want to be absolutely sure that this is the right decision for you.

Celebrate with family and friends

However you decide to celebrate, make sure you take some time out to enjoy yourself with family and friends. After all, it isn't every day that you get asked to join a very exclusive club. You are going to have some tough times ahead as a junior partner, so take the opportunity to enjoy yourself before the honeymoon period finishes.

Thank everyone who has helped you along the journey

Make a list of everyone who has helped you along the journey. Then, ring to thank each person individually. Don't do a mass email.

Arrange your finances to invest capital in your firm

Most mid- to large-sized firms will have arrangements with a bank to provide their new partners with a loan to cover the capital they will need to invest in the firm. However you choose to finance your capital to the firm you need to have it ready by the time you are formally appointed to the partnership.

Sort out your personal financial affairs

On the day you get made up to partner you will have to resign and become self-employed. You will lose all your employment rights and all the employee benefits you have enjoyed will come to an end. This means you need to:

- Find out what benefits your firm provides for its partners and the cost to you of this.

- Potentially start a personal pension

- Sort out your life insurance and alternative suppliers for the employee benefits the firm previously provided you with

- Find out how and when you will be able to access drawings. You may need to organise a short-term loan to cover the gap between when your monthly salary stops and you are able to access your drawings.

- Find out what support your firm offers to help you with your tax affairs now that – if you are in the UK – you will be on self-assessment rather than PAYE for your tax.

Create your PR and communication plan

Making partner is a massive achievement, which becomes a great "good news" story and marketing opportunity. In fact you probably have a window of up to 9 months to exploit numerous PR opportunities in the local, national and trade press just because you are 'hot property' as a new partner.

Before you start to construct your own plan, talk with your marketing and PR team to see what they have already planned for you. After all, you don't want to reinvent the wheel. They can also advise you if the news of you being admitted to the partnership is embargoed.

As a minimum, your PR and communication plan should include:

- How and when you will break the news on social media, particularly LinkedIn and Twitter. Remember you may not be able to change your job status on LinkedIn until after the day you are formally admitted to the partnership.

- How you will contact personally, by phone or in person, all of your A-listers, (see Chapter 9) especially your clients and professional intermediaries, to tell them your good news.

Becoming partner is often a once in a lifetime occurrence; therefore, it makes sense to do more than just the suggested minimum. Which trade publications would you like to appear in? How about thinking about some articles that you could pitch to them?

Build a new 3-year Career Plan

Once you have made it over the line and have approval to be admitted to the partnership, the work doesn't stop there. After all, once you have reached the top of one career ladder, you are then at the bottom of another career ladder! In addition, there is often a sense of anticlimax. After all, making partner is what you may have been striving for since you entered the professions as a trainee fresh out of university.

It is at this point you need an empty piece of paper and build yourself a 3-year Career Plan. This plan can actually be quite illuminating.

The question is, what needs to go into your 3-year Career Plan as a new partner, or soon-to-be-new partner.

Take time out to reflect on what really motivates you

Up until this point in your career you have probably been working very hard to get to partner. Now the pressure has reduced a little, do take the time out to reflect on what you truly want from the next three years, both personally and professionally.

 Use the Career Kitbag's Wheel of Life exercise to help you reflect on what you want from the next three years, both personally and professionally.

If you can, take yourself out of the office and maybe go away for a few days. Let your mind de-stress and let yourself truly unwind, then you will find it much easier to get close to what you really want from the next few years.

Go back and look at your Business Case for partner

Go back to your Business Case for partner. This is one of the places to start looking for what you want or need to achieve professionally. It will give you a steer on the numbers you need to achieve.

Ask yourself, 'What do I want my legacy to be?'

If you had a crystal ball, what would you want to have achieved in the next three years? But more than that, how can you make sure that you positively impact on other people in your new role of partner? What will you do to be part of other peoples' success?

What is going to be different now?

Up until now someone else has called pretty much all of the 'professional' shots for you. (Of course if you are not yet a full equity partner, the situation is not going to change that drastically in the short term.) However, as an owner of the business you get to be master of your own destiny a little more. What will you do that is different and make you and/or the people around you more fulfilled, happier and more successful?

What is your 100-day Action Plan?

It is all very well having grand 3-year Career Plans, but you do need to get started on it today … Therefore, look at your Plan and identify for yourself what is realistic and motivating that you can get done in the next 100 days.

Don't forget you need to 'win work' *and* 'build your team'

All too often the focus as a junior partner can be on 'hitting your numbers'. Remember that if you are going to build a successful career to full equity partner it needs to be more than just the numbers. What proportion of your time will you spend building a team to support your ambitions going forward?

How will you become one of the club?

As mentioned earlier, you are starting to climb another career ladder now that you are a partner. Part of your 3-year Career Plan needs to contain some thoughts on how you will increase your influence, status and equity holding within the partnership. What cross-firm projects, groups or committees do you need to join or lead?

How to pick yourself up if you are unsuccessful in the vote

Firstly, if you are reading this section of the book because you have just been told you are not going to make partner this time around, I feel for you. However expected or unexpected this is for you, you are probably feeling a bit raw now. One of the best ways to move forward after this set back is to realise that cliché about *What doesn't kill you makes you stronger* is true for you *right* now. Having knockbacks is all part of the hurly-burly of being in the professions. The more resilient you can get to these *slings and arrows of outrageous fortune* the more successful you will become.

If it makes you feel any better, it is common for people *not* to get to partner first time around. Your firm may not be able to make up every strong candidate for partnership this time around. Some firms even send candidates through the Partnership Admissions Process before they are ready to 'blood' them, and make them more resilient and ready for the process second time around. However gutted you feel, now is not the time to throw in the towel. Now is the time to:

- Examine your feelings on getting turned down. Are you devastated, ambivalent or secretly relieved? Aim to tap into the cause of your emotion and use that to help you decide on what is the next step for your career.

- Get formal and informal feedback from your Mentor and Sponsoring Partner, on what they believe were the weaknesses in your Business Case and Personal Case that let you down this time around.

- Book some time with your Mentor to help you re-centre yourself

- Keep your head up high and behave with dignity. You probably want to keep doors open for another attempt next year.

It can be tempting to want to immediately move into action mode again to plan your next assault on partnership. You may be better to consciously press *Pause*. After all, your emotions will have been on a roller coaster for definitely the last few months and possibly the last few years. The last thing you want to do is take an irreversible decision, which is being driven by out-of-control emotions. Even if your natural state of affairs is to start planning or take action, I counsel you to actually take some time to reflect. Reflect on the feedback you have received and your reactions to not getting through the vote. Get soundings from your Support Team on what they think you should do next. After all you still have many options available to you; for example,

- Go for partnership next time around

- Look to make partnership in a different firm

- Stay as a director, senior associate or senior manager and forget your partnership ambitions for the short and medium term

- Go into industry

- Consider a career change.

When your head is in the right place again, then it is time to reset your Goals and start the planning process to help you meet these Goals. (See Chapter 1)

Summary

Now that you have reached the end of the Partner Track, it is time to reset your Goals and start the career planning approach again.

Finishing the Partnership Admissions Process can be an emotionally draining time. Therefore, give your head time to clear before you take any major decisions based on the result of the Partnership Vote.

Action Points

1. Organise some time off work to be able to reflect on what are the right next steps for you.

2. Book time with your Mentor and Sponsoring Partner to discuss what happens next.

3. If you were successful at the Vote

   1. Finish your due diligence on yourself and the firm

   2. Organise your personal financial affairs

   3. Write your PR and communications plan to let your network and marketplace know about your admission to the partnership

4. Spend time with your family and friends to discuss the implications of the Partnership Vote for you and others.

Further resources

WEBSITES

- Free guide to *Making a success of your first 12 months as a partner* and details of Executive Coaches who can help you successfully make the transition to partnership: http://www.howtomakepartner.com

What now?

I've waffled for long enough. It's now time for you to take action on your intention of making it to partner.

If you haven't already, go to How to make partner, http://www. howtomakepartner.com and access resources from the Career Kitbag.

I'd love to know how you are getting along on your career journey to making partner AND what you thought of this book.

Go on, send me an email at Heather@heathertownsend.co.uk or send me a tweet at @heathertowns or connect with me on LinkedIn,

If you have liked this book please leave a short review on Amazon and GoodReads. You will make my day!

About Heather Townsend

Heather is always up for a challenge. Perhaps this is why she specialises in, predominantly, helping accountants, lawyers & consultants create work-winning conversations with new clients. You know, the really difficult bit, how to actually kick the door down to get a meeting with a potential client.

In fact, over the last 12 months Heather has supported her clients to build their profile, differentiate themselves, grow their reputation, and in the process add over £1 million in fees to their client portfolio.

When Heather is not writing, speaking or coaching she can found increasing her waist line with her homemade gluten and dairy free cakes.

Accolades and endorsements include:

1. Economia, magazine of the Institute of Chartered Accountants of England and Wales, decided Heather was in the top 50 influencers on finance & business on social media in 2013 and 2014.

2. So far 100% of the people who Heather has coached or supported for over 6 months to help make partner have gone on to make partner

3. Judging the Practice Excellence Awards in 2015 and the British Accountancy Awards in 2011 and 2012

4. Publishing 3 books with Financial Times Publishing and Kogan Page, which have collectively been translated into over 7 different languages, sold over 20,000 copies and received over 150 five star reviews on Amazon.

Who Heather works with:

Her work splits into 4 distinctive areas:

1. Helping high potential accountants, lawyers and consultants build a cast-iron business and personal case to help them make partner in their firm

2. Working with owners of small professional practices, often under 4 equity partners, or intact sector teams radically increase their new client leads and wins without resorting to cold calling

3. Helping business book authors grow their business through writing their own book.

4. Helping students and alumni of business schools achieve their career and business goals via their network and networking activities

Heather features regularly in the national & trade press, e.g. FT, Guardian, Sunday Times, Managing Partner, Legal Week, Accountancy Age.

To work with Heather

To contact Heather about working together:

Heather can be contacted via email,
heather@heathertownsend.co.uk

or

+44 (0) 1234 48 0123

Other books written by the author

The FT Guide To Business Networking

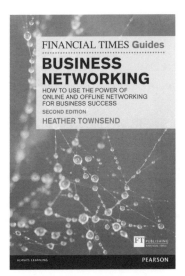

The book is now in its 2nd edition and has been translated into 5 different languages, been awarded over 110 five star reviews on amazon and sold over 13000 copies globally.

Up to 80 per cent of opportunities come from people who already know you, so the more people you know, the more chance you have of winning the new business or career you want.

The Financial Times Guide to Business Networking is your definitive introduction to a joined-up networking strategy that really works. This award-winning book has now been fully updated to include new chapters on generating referrals and boosting your confidence when networking, as well as the latest advice on social networking sites.

Discover:

- Successfully combine online and offline networking techniques
- Develop the best networking approaches and behaviours
- Make a great first impression, build rapport and generate strong business relationships
- Talk to the right people, have productive conversations and effectively work a room

❝ 'A great, practical guide to all aspects of networking – stuffed with lots of quick and easy tips to help you leverage the power of your network.'

IVAN MISNER, NY TIMES BESTSELLING AUTHOR AND FOUNDER OF BNI AND REFERRAL INSTITUTE

❝ 'This practical and easy-to-read book will quickly get you the results you need from your network.'

CHARLIE LAWSON, BNI UK AND IRELAND NATIONAL DIRECTOR

❝ 'A "must read" for anyone wanting to use the power of face-to-face AND online networking to generate career and business success.'

ANDY LOPATA, AUTHOR OF RECOMMENDED AND AND DEATH CAME THIRD

How to make partner and still have a life

(co-authored with Jo Larbie)

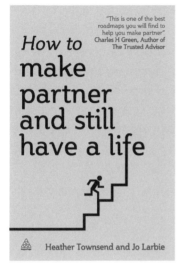

The book has now sold over 4000 copies globally and gained 15 five star reviews on Amazon.

The burning question on every ambitious fee-earner's lips is: 'how do I make partner at this firm?' This book is your route map to making it to the top in a professional services firm. It shows you how to stand out, be in the right place at the right time and build your kitbag of skills to overcome the many hurdles and reach the Holy Grail of becoming partner. This book reveals what it really takes to make it, and what it will involve once you're there. It helps you make an informed decision on whether or not this is the right step for you, and guides you on how to become a partner and still have a life of your own. Heather Townsend and Jo Larbie show you the rules of the game, laying bare exactly what you need to do to take the ultimate step.

❮❮ I wish I'd had access to a book like this before I became a partner."

CHARLES H GREEN, AUTHOR OF THE TRUSTED ADVISOR

❮❮ If you have aspirations to make Partner and you only purchase one book this year - make this that one. It could quite literally change your life."

DREW MOSS, HEAD OF LEARNING AND DEVELOPMENT, BDO AUSTRALIA

((Another must-have read from Heather Townsend. A book that looks at the reality of what it is to be a Partner and provides essential practical advice for anyone considering promotion."

CLAIRE MARTIN, DIRECTOR TYNDALLWOODS

((The book is an excellent study of the professional services world and the increasingly high demands on partners. Its reach is beyond the practical career roadmap and how-to-do-it guidance which is very helpful. The authors firmly believe that success in business can be achieved without sacrificing the quality of your personal life. It is all about making the right choices and getting all the support along this long journey.

FILIP LYAPOV, SENIOR AUDIT MANAGER EY

The Go-To Expert

The Go-To Expert has 40+ five star reviews on amazon and has now sold over 4000 copies globally.

The Go-To Expert provides no-nonsense advice on managing your transition into a well-known and trusted name within your industry. It will help you navigate reputation-building tools with confidence and build a personal brand that wins you business.

Discover:

- Simple steps to raise your profile
- How to market and sell yourself with ease and confidence
- Techniques to make your clients come to you

If you want to move your career on, shifting from being just another professional advisor to being truly recognised as a go-to expert, this book will show you the way."

RICHARD NEWTON, AWARD-WINNING AUTHOR OF THE MANAGEMENT BOOK

Differentiating yourself from your peers is the challenge that every professional faces. This book gives you the clarity, process and confidence to make yourself stand out in a crowded market place."

TONI HUNTER, PARTNER, GEORGE HAY CHARTERED ACCOUNTANTS

" The Go-To-Expert is an inspirational guide for accountants, law-yers and consultants who wish to develop their niche special-ism. Packed with great ideas and insights, it enables you, the reader, to undertake the journey through a series of exercises, each building on the next, to create your proposition and tacti-cal marketing plan for your target clients. I cannot recommend it highly enough - it will help and inspire you to become the Go-To-Expert."

PHIL MULLIS, PARTNER WILKINS KENNEDY

" Having read the book from cover to cover and now about to re-read it my key takeaway was the reinforcement of defining and promoting a niche. Becoming a Go To Expert in a specialist field. I knew I should do it but just not got round to it. It is now a prior-ity of mine, something I shall focus on over the next few months. The book is an education in itself with many practical examples based on real life professionals. It is a must for any one in a pro-fessional career that wants to get ahead."

PAUL ANTHONY MILLER

" I found this book a really excellent step by step guide for profes-sionals seeking to develop expert status. While it contains very good advice for strategic planning, it also provides very specific useful tactical tips on exactly how to go about things like net-working and blogging in a very targeted way.

This book provides a blueprint for practice and personal develop-ment for professionals."

FLOR MCCARTHY, AUTHOR OF THE SOLICITOR'S GUIDE TO
MARKETING AND GROWING A BUSINESS